Don Troiani's

AMERICAN
BATTLES

Don Troiani's
AMERICAN BATTLES

THE ART OF THE NATION AT WAR, 1754–1865

Art by Don Troiani

Text by Robert K. Krick, Keith Knoke, Lee White, Robert E. L. Krick, Dr. Richard Sauers, James L. Kochan, Bob McDonald, Jay Jorgensen, Dr. David Evans, and Brian Pohanka

Foreword by Peter Harrington

Additional contributors:
Howard Michael Madaus, Eric J. Wittenburg, A. M. Gambone, Kathy G. Harrison, Lawrence F. Kohl, William Erquitt, Keith Gibson, Lance J. Herdegen, Christopher M. Calkins, Stephen W. Sears, A. Wilson Green, Anthony Wayne Tommel

STACKPOLE
BOOKS

Copyright © 2006 by Stackpole Books
Images © 2006 by Don Troiani

First published in paperback in 2013 by
STACKPOLE BOOKS
5067 Ritter Road
Mechanicsburg, PA 17055
www.stackpolebooks.com

Printed in China

10   9   8   7   6   5   4   3   2   1

FIRST PAPERBACK EDITION

ISBN-13: 978-0-8117-1274-3 (paperback)
ISBN-10: 0-8117-1274-5 (paperback)

For free information about the artwork and limited edition prints of Don Troiani, contact:
Historical Art Prints
P.O. Box 660
Southbury, CT 06488
203-262-6680
www.historicalartprints.com

For information on licensing images in this book, visit www.historicalimagebank.com

Cover design by Tracy Patterson
Front cover art: *"Emmitsburg Road"*

Library of Congress Cataloging-in-Publication Data

Troiani, Don.
    Don Troiani's American battles : the art of the nation at war, 1754–1865 / art by Don Troiani ;
text by Robert K. Krick ... [et al.] ; foreword by Peter Harrington ; additional contributors,
Howard Michael Madaus ... [et al.].— 1st ed.
        p. cm.
    ISBN-13: 978-0-8117-3327-4
    ISBN-10: 0-8117-3327-0
    1. United States—History, Military—Pictorial works. 2. Battles—United States—Pictorial works.
    3. Soldiers—United States—Pictorial works. 4. War in art. I. Krick, Robert K. II. Title.

E181.T85 2006
355.4'7309033—dc22
                                                2006003646

To my father,
Dominick H. Troiani (1916–2005),
who always took an interest in everything I did,

AND

to my friend and historian
Brian Pohanka (1955–2005).

Extras for the 2003 film Cold Mountain. *Don Troiani served as a consultant to the movie's costumers and prop makers, guiding the re-creation of Civil War uniforms, equipment, and flags.* PHOTO BY MICHAEL KRAUS

CONTENTS

Foreword

ix

Acknowledgments

xiii

Introduction

xiv

Don Troiani in the midst of his hand-picked models.

A Legacy of Military Art

[It] represented an episode of stubborn fighting in some battle of the Civil War. A broken line or group of Union soldiers, evidently hard pressed, was seen facing—if I recollect rightly—the spectator, who thus occupied the position of the supposed attacking force. The attack was not shown in the picture, or at most was barely indicated. The defenders were the whole subject: they only were placed before us, powder-stained, resolute, firing, reloading, or grasping their weapons in expectancy of closer combat, and evidently determined to sell their lives dearly or retreat only when overpowered. From the presentation of this one side of the fight, the other side could be realized easily and with great intensity. The picture, therefore, in addition to its merits of drawing, painting, vividness, and character, was a fine instance of imaginative power, and also of the power of exciting imagination in the beholder.

This description of a painting by Gilbert Gaul appeared in 1893, but it could equally describe any of Don Troiani's works. He follows a long line of gifted artists of war that stretches back more than a millennium. In placing Troiani's art in its historical context, it is useful to survey the history of war art from earliest times to the present. We can then better understand the significance and relevance of Troiani's paintings of soldiers in battle.

Ever since man has fought his fellow man, their acts have been portrayed in visual forms. Some of the earliest cave paintings depict tribal warfare. The representation of armed conflict became more formalized in ancient Middle and Near Eastern societies with their illustrations of the victories of the Egyptians and Assyrians. In numerous carved monuments such as the bas-reliefs of Rameses I and Seti I at Karnac and of Assurbanipal at Nimroud (Nineva), we see larger-than-life leaders riding chariots over their conquered enemies. There was little respect for reality since glorification was the primary motivation behind such art, as it was in the subsequent classical empires. In the column commemorating the Emperor Trajan's victories near the forum in Rome, we see a detailed frieze portraying the armies of the empire defeating the Dacians. The stonemasons who crafted those sculptures clearly depicted the costumes and weapons of the combatants in a way that has informed historians to this day.

However, it would be well over another millennium before such detail appeared in war art. In the intermediate period, the form of artistic representation became more stylized. One thinks particularly of the Bayeux Tapestry, which shows a military campaign—in this case, the Norman conquest of Britain in 1066—in the form of a narrative cartoon strip that follows the course of events from beginning to end. The panorama guides us to the kinds of weaponry and clothing worn by the Norman knights and Saxon housecarls. Once again, the aim of the creators was to glorify the victor, here William of Normandy, but also to create a visual record of the achievement for the citizens of Normandy. Similarly, medieval illuminated manuscripts portrayed war in a schematic fashion with little regard for accuracy in detail.

In the art of the Renaissance, war does not figure prominently, although the two most renowned artists, Leonardo Da Vinci and Michelangelo, each included images of war in their *oeuvre*. Later still, in the intriguing triptych chronicling the Tuscan battle of San Romano in 1432, the Florentine painter Paolo Uccello painted the actors in this brief event as though they were participants in a medieval pageant. The leaders of the opposing sides are arrayed in tournament style ready to joust. The artist was clearly aware of the costume, weapons, armor, and horse trappings of the period, right down to a crossbowman drawing back the string of his weapon. Uccello was also very familiar with the landscape of the surrounding area, even though it is represented as a standardized backdrop. Nonetheless, we can point to the San Romano series as representing the genesis of the formal battle painting.

Two centuries later, it was the portrayal of the surrender of Breda in 1623 by the great Spanish painter Velázquez that provided a continuum from Uccello. In this costume drama, we see the chief characters in the formal act of surrender. Europe was embroiled in almost continuous warfare, and society was well acquainted with war and its attendant horrors. Velázquez chose instead to focus on the honor of war as the defeated Spanish general humbly offers his sword to the noble victor. In contrast, the French artist Jacques Callot had none of that. For him, a veteran of the fighting in Lorraine during the Thirty Years' War, human conflict was not something to represent kindly. The viewer will not find glowing color in his pictures, nor careful delineation of weapons or costume. War in Callot's eyes is anonymous; there are no victors or losers, only perpetrators and victims. For him, war was universal, involving everyone not just soldiers. He wanted to record and condemn the horrors of war. He had seen fighting firsthand and wanted no part in its glorification.

It would be another century before artists began to choose war for its intrinsic value rather than merely chronicling it. Out of the Enlightenment came the concept of the military hero. Earlier, the Duke of Marlborough and his generals had commissioned rich tapestries recording their successes in the War of the Spanish Succession. The French artist Antoine Watteau depicted the life of soldiers in the first part of the eighteenth century, but it took another few decades before the military epic emerged as a unique form of artistic expression. In particular, the "death tableaux" mirrored the concept of heroism on the battlefield. The leading proponents of this genre were the American trio of Benjamin West, John Singleton Copley, and John Trumbull. Practicing their trade in a London burgeoning from the wealth of the empire, West, Copley, and, to a lesser extent, Trumbull took advantage of the prevailing popularity of the army that was anchoring the colonial enterprises. Even with the loss of the American colonies, the officer class still commanded high respect in society. With celebrated paintings such as the *Death of General Wolfe*, the *Death of Major Pierson*, and the *Sortie from Gibraltar* by the three artists respectively, they strove for detail and accuracy amid historical narratives that were occasionally suspect. The success of these works inspired others to emulate them and create spectacular historical tableaux rich in detail. One thinks in particular of the stage like works of P. J. de Loutherbourg and Robert Ker Porter, who went to great lengths to capture realism. Their dramatic paintings, often created in panoramic fashion, were crammed with detailed vignettes. To achieve such accuracy, they sought out eyewitnesses, obtained samples of clothing, and sometimes visited the actual scenes of their epics. They were laying the groundwork for a succession of artists who would emerge to the forefront a century later. Indeed, Troiani himself can be said to be following in their footsteps.

The Napoleonic Wars were a watershed in military art, providing opportunities for many craftsmen and artisans. In the France of Napoleon, artists were sought out to chronicle the successes of the army. Later, competitions were held for the best renditions of certain battles, and it was to one of these contests that Antoine-Jean Gros submitted his winning 1807 cartoon of the battle of Eylau that resulted in the cele-brated canvas that hangs today in the Louvre. Crammed with detail of uniforms and accoutrements, Gros's painting and others by his contemporary Louis François Lejeune provide a visual record of the victories of the empire, albeit with some artistic license for the truth. But in a state where censorship of that truth was rampant, the artists played the game. The wars even saw the appearance of official artists in a small way. War art was seen as a mechanism for establishing reputations, cementing power, and perpetuating ambition. State-sanctioned art emerged and continued to be a factor in war paintings throughout the nineteenth and twentieth centuries. Even so, realism was not compromised, and artists still enriched their canvases with rich details of uniforms, weaponry, and landscape even though battles were often depicted in a distant panoramic fashion. It was not all glory, however, as Francisco Goya's seminal series, *The Horrors of War*, all too graphically proclaimed.

Even with his death, Napoleon was still lionized in art by his countrymen. One thinks of the great Horace Vernet and the massive paintings hanging in the Galerie de Batailles at Versailles. Commissioned by Louis Philippe in the 1830s, they were intended to remind the French of their glorious martial past and connect the current ruler with the great emperor. Realism was the order of the day, and once again, the artists went to great lengths to accurately record the image of soldiers in battle. It was the era of romanticism, and pictures of war beyond officially sanctioned works offered artists a means of depicting human emotions at their extreme. Eugene Delacroix's wonderfully vivid costume drama of 1824, *The Massacre of Chios*, captured the horror and suffering of humans in conflict but expressed them in idealized terms.

Military art in the middle of the nineteenth century was dominated by the work of Adolf Menzel, the great Prussian artist who created the enduring image of Frederick the Great in battle, as well as scenes from Waterloo and the German wars of unification. One thinks, for instance, of *The Night at Hochkirch*, a life-size depiction of the night of October 14–15, 1758, when the fate of the Prussians seemed hopeless as the Austrians began closing in. King Frederick suddenly appeared, took command, and urged his men on to victory. For Menzel, such moments, such incidents, were more important than creating the whole event in one picture. This approach of focusing on a part rather than the whole became his guiding principle. As one critic noted in 1895, "in a word, [Menzel] is a realist to whom the actual factors of a group count for more than its general effect. The uniforms and the decorations of the officers, the harness of the horses, are to him as important as if they were historical documents liable to be consulted by any future student of the time." As another writer commented four years earlier, "it was not sufficient for him to sketch an object in the view he wished to give of it, but he must draw a gun, a sword, a *porte-épée*, a saddle, from two, three, four, and even five different points of view, making himself so accurately acquainted with the object that in his mind he seemed to have it before him in plastic form." Always striving for verisimilitude, Menzel himself had never actually witnessed combat firsthand and had always wondered how accurate his depictions of war really were. The opportunity to answer that question came in 1866 when he visited the battlefield of Sadowa just after the overwhelming victory of the Prussians over the Austrians. Viewing the dead, he was able to satisfy himself that his imaginary portrayals of the victims of battle were indeed quite accurate.

Elsewhere, other artists began focusing on the incident instead of the whole event. Elizabeth Thompson, better known as Lady Butler, in Britain and Ernest Meissonier in France created striking expressions of soldiers caught in the moment or aftermath of battle. Thompson's Crimean trilogy of *The Roll Call, Balaclava,* and *The Return from Inkermann* was quite a departure from the norm. Here, for the first time, in Britain were depictions of the true face of war—the dirt, the suffering, the pain and anguish of defeat or victory. Nonetheless, at the same time that her paintings were making the rounds of the Royal Academy in the 1870s and 1880s, popular entertainments still included vast 360-degree canvases encompassing every detail of battle in panoramic style. Such vast circular paintings constantly attracted crowds in Europe and America, highlighting the battles of the Crimean War, the American Civil War, and the Franco-Prussian War.

During the last decades of the nineteenth century, battle art achieved its pinnacle of greatness, and the canvases that came out of this period have provided the inspiration that has motivated Don Troiani ever since he began painting images of war. Just as we have identified the trio of American painters—West, Copley, and Trumbull—who created great masterpieces of war art in the late eighteenth century, so too can we identify another threesome, this one French, working a century later. Meissonier, Edouard Détaille, and Alphonse de Neuville created some of the greatest paintings of the French at war. They were not alone, however, for ever since the days of Napoleon and Louis Philippe, French artists showed a penchant for things military. Indeed, the Salon Militaire attracted some of France's finest painters in the decades prior to the Great War. Significantly, many sought the disaster of the war with Prussia in 1870–71 for their artistic inspiration, and countless paintings appeared on the walls of the Salon and elsewhere, capturing the heroics of the lost cause. Indeed, it has even been suggested that the French artists won on canvas what the French army lost in the field.

While French battle art overshadows much of the war art that came from other countries, there were a number of equally important artists working in the genre outside of France. Just as the French had a long tradition of depicting their armies, so too did the Germans. Unlike Britain, for example, royal patronage was common, and many artists were encouraged to accompany the armies in the wars of unification against Denmark, Austria, and France. Competitions were even held for the best portrayals of certain victories. Anton von Werner, Wilhelm Camphausen, Georg Bleibtrau, Emil Hünten, and many others built their reputations painting the glories of Prussian and German arms.

Troiani himself often singles out the work of another great German war artist, Carl Röchling. Born near Saarbruck in 1855, he is regarded as perhaps the most prolific military artist of late nineteenth-century Germany. He studied under von Werner in 1880 and understandably was drawn to military subjects. The events of the Franco-Prussian War were particularly appealing to the young artist, and he produced a steady stream of paintings showing the victorious Prussians in battle. Historical battles also appear among his *oeuvre,* and surprisingly, he painted a large scene of the American Civil War battle of Fredericksburg. In fact, he had to obtain special permission from the German emperor since much of his work at the time was on commission for the royal family. In October 1899, the emperor himself visited Röchling's studio to view the nearly completed Fredericksburg picture and expressed great admiration for it. Apparently, he spent more than an hour examining the canvas. The artist lived to see the Great War, dying in Berlin in 1920 but not before leaving a rich legacy of paintings and illustrations commemorating German military successes.

Artists like Détaille, Röchling, and the British painters Ernest Crofts, William Barnes Wollen, and Richard Caton Woodville surrounded themselves with countless original artifacts, weapons, and accoutrements in order to achieve accuracy in their pictures. They visited the scenes of the action, interviewed the participants, and made every effort to capture the event in the minutest detail. Working a century later, Troiani continues this tradition and is committed to creating works full of detail.

While looking to European artists mainly for motivation, Troiani relies on other American painters as an impetus for his work. Troiani's Civil War paintings, for instance, echo the works of Julian Scott and Gilbert Gaul, who both practiced their craft in the decades following the Civil War and had access to veterans and contemporary artifacts. And so we return to Gilbert Gaul. A list of Gilbert Gaul's paintings could easily be titles of Troiani's canvases: *Charging the Battery* (1882), *The Wounded Officer* (both exhibited at the Paris Universal Exhibition of 1889), *Charging an Earthwork* (1888), and *Holding the Line at All Hazards* (1881). In *On Dangerous Ground,* exhibited at the National Academy in 1889, we see Union troops hiding behind a haystack while others are being shot at; his painting entitled *Bringing Up the Guns* would be equally at home in any exhibit of French military art.

Born in the same year as Röchling, Gaul in his lifetime established a reputation as one of the greatest painters and illustrators of the American soldier. He was considered by many to be the Détaille of America. In an interview with the artist published in 1898, the writer stated that none of Gaul's pictures were "studio" pictures:

> *All his sketches are made from life out on the frontier, where he has lived at the army posts for months at a time. Of course he does not paint his pictures out in the open; he uses a camera and a color-box, and makes his notes from life, but paints his picture in his studio, where he has enough old uniforms to fit out an awkward squad. Indeed, his whole house has a military appearance, for swords are crossed over the drawing-room mantelpiece, and the center-piece of the dining-room ceiling is made of muskets grouped so as to form a circle. The old uniforms are, however, relegated to the studio, which is on the second floor. There, there are more swords and muskets, and a half-fin-ished battle picture stands upon the easel.*

In an assessment of the military art of the twentieth century, the world wars naturally dominate. The official war artists of the time stressed the experience rather than the detail. There were, as well, artists of historical battles who were still plying their art. At the beginning of the century, Howard Pyle and later some of his students, including Frank Schoonover,

Gayle Porter Hoskins, and N. C. Wyeth, established careers by creating enduring scenes of historical events from the nation's history. Although much of their work was for illustrations in various magazines and weeklies, this does not detract from their craftsmanship. In their battle scenes, they focused, like Troiani and others before them, on a moment in battle. Pyle's celebrated painting, *The Whites of Their Eyes*, portrays the advance of the British redcoats up Breed's Hill in 1775, while his canvas for an illustration in *Harper's Magazine* in 1909 enti-tled *They Awaited the Order to Charge* captures the moment when young Union soldiers sit restlessly below a bank as their commanders decide their fate. One soldier in the foreground looks forlorn as he awaits the order.

Artists such as Röchling, Détaille, Gaul, and Pyle in the past, and Troiani today, realize they can never possibly achieve the true reality of men in battle. What they do so well is give us an idea, a sense of what these battles might have been like. They show us the weapons being fired, the cumbersome uniforms and accoutrements, the conditions the men encountered, the terrain, the weather, all created from a true knowledge of those factors based on endless hours of research. The fruits of their labors remain as lasting impres-sions of some of the great moments in history.

Peter Harrington
Curator, Anne S. K. Brown Military Collection
Brown University Library

ACKNOWLEDGMENTS

I am grateful for the assistance and support of the following people: Herman Benninghoff, William L. Brown III, Christopher Bryant, Charles Childs, Rene Chartrand, Ed Christopher, Earl J. Coates, Candee Cochran, Henry Cooke, Dr. David Evans, Elaine Duillo, the late John Duillo, Mary Evans, Robin Feret, Scott Ferriss, James C. Frasca, Joe Fulginiti, Fred Gaede, Al M. Gambone, William Gladstone, Erik Goldstein, Bruce Herman, Steve Hill, Seth Hopkins, The Horse Soldier Shop, Keith Knoke, Jay Jorgenson, Mark Jaeger, Les Jensen, James L. Kochan, Paul C. Loane, Michael J. McAfee, Bob McDonald, Edward J. Magee, Howard M. Madaus, Col. J. Craig Nannos, Dean Nelson, John Ockerbloom, Donna O'Brien, Michael O'Donnell, Ken Osen, the late Brian Pohanka, Cricket Pohanka, John Rees, Steve Rogers, Dr. Richard Sauers, Eric Schnitzer, Greg Starbuck, David Sullivan, Bill Synomon, Brendan Synomon, Jessica Troiani, Ed Vebell, Anthony Wayne Tommel, Ron Tunison, Richard Ulbrich, Lee White, and Tim Wilson.

If I have inadvertently excluded anyone, please accept my apologies.

Don Troiani
Southbury, Connecticut

INTRODUCTION

The paintings in this book represent not only twenty-five years of my life, but also a childhood spent listening to my father's colorful stories about his experiences in the 358th Field Artillery, 95th Infantry Division, during World War II and collecting the real objects of war.

My interest in art began early. I drew at home and, while teachers droned in front of the blackboard, at school. My notebooks were fully illustrated with vivid Napoleonic battles—and occasionally even schoolwork. With barely passing grades, a "good" college was out of the question, which was fine with me since I had wanted to go to art school all along. The Pennsylvania Academy of Fine Art in Philadelphia was my first choice, and it accepted my portfolio, undoubtedly the only one consisting entirely of military subject matter. Even the required self-portrait was painted in the uniform of a French Napoleonic marshal.

Disappointingly, while art school was enjoyable, there was practically no emphasis on old-style academic training. For the most part, students were permitted to do their own thing, and criticism, considered destructive of one's creativity, was watered down in order not to crush any inflated egos. Fortunately for me, there were still a few old realist teachers on the staff, like Oliver Grimley and Walter Stumfig, who were trained in the traditional manner and took a personal interest in me. I learned a great deal from both of these fine gentlemen, who sharply critiqued my pathetic scrawlings on a regular basis. The art museum at the school was also superb, having the works of many of the old greats such as Eakins, Homer, West, and others. The learning experience was unequalled as I skipped class and closely examined the work of the masters for countless hours.

After art school, I quickly got assignments from *American Heritage* magazine, as well as from the National Park Service, which was getting ready for the bicentennial of the American Revolution. Early on, through collecting, I met famed illustrator Ed Vebell, who had been an artist for *Stars and Stripes* magazine during World War II. Ed taught me much about drawing and painting that I would not have figured out otherwise.

My father in Germany, 1944–45.

Dressing actors for a scene in the History Channel's "Civil War Journal."

In the early 1980s, the Society of American Historical Artists was formed, with my Stamford apartment functioning as the meeting place for our quarterly get-togethers. At the meetings, each artist displayed his work for a critique of its historical and artistic merits. During the discussion, the submitter was not allowed to defend his piece, but dutifully had to listen to, and endure, the frequently scathing criticism. It turned out to be one of the most refreshing experiences of my career.

In addition to art school and fellow artists, my interest in collecting military artifacts has also been useful to my painting. My passion for collecting began on a trip to Paris with my parents in the early 1960s. One day, we passed a shop selling militaria. Despite having almost no money, I was still determined to buy something. I finally settled on a plain German World War II helmet for the sucker tourist price of seven dollars. However cheap the cost, the excitement of actually owning this commonplace item was an experience I will always remember. My mind visualized the great battles the helmet might have been worn in, and even better, it now belonged to me. Since then, I have always thought it was extraordinary that individuals can own items that should—or at least could—be in museums.

When I was a child, one of my elementary school friends had a summer home on Lake George, where we were told we could find old muskets in the woods—an obvious fabrication but one credible enough to fuel an early interest in digging for colonial artifacts. Later, after reading *History Writ-*

ten with Pick and Shovel, a series of archeological reports of digs by the New York Historical Society in the 1920s, I realized, that they had been digging within driving distance of my house. The hunt was on. Teaming up with my father and equipped with a primitive metal detector, I set out to one of the sites. Within moments, I found a cannonball and a pewter spoon. Thus was launched a relic-hunting career of more than thirty years. Combing sites along the Hudson, Lake George, Lake Champlain, and even down to the Caribbean, I collected an impressive array of objects. Most importantly, I also gained valuable insight into not only the artifacts but also the soldier life of the era.

Around 1969, I met Craig Nannos and joined the 43rd Regiment of Foot/2nd Pennsylvania reenactment unit, in

With Joe Fulginiti, Donna, and historians Dennis Fry and Brian Pohanka.

With models for "Civil War Journal."

which I was active until about 1980. I formed friendships with other students of the colonial and Civil War eras, including Paul Loane, William L. Brown III, Jerry Coates, Frank Kravic, George Neuman, and many others who remain friends to this day. In 1982, I met Jim Kochan, a consummate student of early military uniforms and equipment. With his exhaustive research and my art skills, we formed a perfect alliance that has endured for two decades. We have collaborated to re-create the soldiers of America's past as they have never been seen before. We have had numerous phone conversations and exchanged countless e-mails, discussing the most trivial of details—such as the tailoring work on a soldier's coat—that even the most learned military historian might not notice.

Sadly, despite the vast research materials readily available, there is probably more grossly inaccurate Civil War painting being done today than at any time since 1865. Uncaring and unknowing artists present their historical fantasy works—advertised as well-researched history—to a trusting public that accepts these erroneous depictions as fact. Everyone makes mistakes; I surely do. However, it is my responsibility to make my paintings as accurate as possible. I don't believe the common excuse that the overall feeling of the piece is more important than the minute historical details. A painting can be both dramatic and accurate. This standard has guided my work for more than three decades.

Digging for Revolutionary War artifacts in the Hudson River valley about 1969.

Artist and U.S. Mint officials stamp out the first of the Civil War battle preservation coins at the Philadelphia Mint.

Receiving the Meritorious Service Award from the U.S. Army National Guard Bureau.

Relic hunting in the Caribbean with Keith Melton and Sam Ellis about 1976.

The Colonial Period, 1636–1775

First Muster

On December 13, 1636, the Massachusetts Bay Colony authorized all males between the ages of sixteen and sixty to be formed into three regiments of militia for the defense of the colony. Here we see the East Regiment at Salem drilling for the first time. Salem is considered to be the birthplace of the U.S. Army National Guard.

ARTIST COMMENTS

This painting was commissioned by the U.S. Army National Guard and was a bit of a challenge for me, as it dealt with an era I was not terribly familiar with. It required a serious seventeenth-century cramming session to study period paintings and armor. The late expert leather artisan Chris Schriber straightaway made me at least one buff coat and some basic accoutrements. Fortunately, long-time friend Frank Kravic had an extensive collection of seventeenth-century weaponry and armor, which was used with the models at his house. Frank, who absolutely looked the part, posed as the instructor, dressed completely in original armor from his collection. The snoopy cat ambled into the shoot, and it looked natural, so I painted him in. Since we were using only a few basic outfits, the models could only be done two at a time. I managed to get a few more models with their own outfits at Plimoth Plantation, which also served as the background.

British Grenadier, 44th Regiment of Foot, 1755.

BRUCE B. HERMAN

Soldier of the Virginia Regiment, 1754.

COL. J. CRAIG NANNOS

Broadsword of the Black Watch, 1759.

Eastern Woodland Indian, 1755–80.

THE BATTLE OF BUSHY RUN:
THE "SWING ACTION" OF AUGUST 6, 1763

In May 1763, the uneasy peace on the trans-Appalachian frontier was broken by a series of coordinated Indian attacks that successfully took most of the British forts in the region, although Forts Pitt and Ligonier in western Pennsylvania successfully held out—but supplies were running low. It was not until late July that Col. Henry Bouquet was able to march westward with a relief column, principally composed of the shattered remnants of two Highland regiments: the 42nd and 77th Foot. By midday of August 5, they were only twenty-six miles from Fort Pitt. Bouquet planned to rest his men at the abandoned station of Bushy Run a mile away before attempting a night march across "a very danger-

ous defile . . . commanded by high and craggy hills." But his careful precautions were to no avail: Gunfire and war cries announced the ambush of Bouquet's advance guard. The Indians were masters of forest warfare and masked their inferior numbers by lightning-quick attacks and careful use of cover. The Highland light infantry moved up quickly to drive them back beyond the ambush point. But as soon as the counterattack halted, the warriors were back, sniping at the regulars from advantageous positions on commanding ground. Each time the regulars fired or charged, the Indians disappeared among the trees, only to reappear at some other point along the column. Bouquet's force, suffering heavy

Minuteman, 1775.

casualties, fell back to the upper slope of Edge Hill, where it formed a circular defense perimeter.

Night brought a temporary cessation to the desperate action, during which Bouquet crafted a daring ploy that would either save his men or irrevocably sign their death warrants. At dawn, the Indians began a loud clamor, howling at and taunting the British. Under cover of a well-directed fire, the attack started anew as parties of warriors attempted to break through the defensive line at various points. The British regulars were tiring, and the fearsome warriors, "besmeared with black and red paint, and covered with the blood of the slain," became even more audacious and pressed home their attack on all sides. Suddenly, two "light" companies pulled out, apparently in retreat, the companies to the right and left of them extending their already-thin lines to fill the space left by the withdrawing troops. As the Indians, now certain of success, increased their fire and the ferocity of their attack, the "retreating" light infantry reappeared at the eastern perimeter. Sallying out, they reached the base of the hill and faced right, forming a two-rank line in open order. With their right flank serving as an anchor, the Scots charged southward in pendulum fashion. Firing a volley, they pressed home their attack with a bayonet charge and pushed the Indians from their cover. As the line swung farther, the Indians to its front were hit by flanking fire from two flank companies, which had been waiting in ambush for this maneuver—seemingly forgotten. Springing up, they joined in a charge that succeeded in rolling up the Indians' right flank and dispersing the warriors. Bouquet's gamble had paid off, wresting victory from apparent defeat.

JAMES L. KOCHAN

Lexington Green, April 19, 1775.

ARTIST COMMENTS

The Highlanders' uniforms had to be made especially for the project, and it was a time-consuming task. Many of the components were crafted by different individuals, all of whom needed to deliver about the same time. Jim Kochan's access to the original orderly books of the regiment provided critical primary data on the appearance of our Highlanders. By 1760, the facings of the Royal Highland Regiment had changed from buff to dark blue, and lapels had been added to the coats. As usual, the models were posed holding original firearms and broadswords from my collection. I was also fortunate in being able to locate some models of Scottish descent that still looked the part of their noble ancestors.

British Grenadier,
38th Regiment of Foot, 1775.

BRUCE B. HERMAN

WILLIAM RODEN

Battalion Soldier of the
29th Regiment of Foot, 1770.

British cartridge box and waistbelt.

TROIANI COLLECTION

The Revolution, 1775–1783

BUNKER HILL

"The danger we were in made us think ... that we were brought there to be all slain ... for about 5 in the morning, we not having more than half our fort done, they began to fire." Thus wrote Pvt. Peter Brown to his mother the week following the momentous June 17, 1775. The night's work had produced a respectable redoubt and connecting breastworks. Intermittently, while the morning's work continued, British warships blasted the Charlestown Peninsula; although generally falling short of the fortifications, the gunnery set the old town ablaze. Half a mile across the bay, thousands of Boston residents watching from rooftops marveled at the destruction. By 1 P.M., they had also witnessed forty barges deliver about 2,200 British troops to that smoky shore.

In the scene shown here, about an hour later, the redoubt's garrison had withstood two massed frontal assaults, inflicting enormous casualties. Each time, His Majesty's regulars performed with remarkable fortitude, overcoming through sheer will the burdens of sixty pounds of gear per man. And each time, the New Englanders reserved their fire almost to the literal point of Col. William Prescott's "whites of their eyes" admonition. Now, though, piling knapsacks at the base of the hill and affixing bayonets, the redcoats were preparing to drive forward in irresistible, savage rage. For not a few of the now greatly outnumbered Yankees atop the hill, the cartridge just loaded was their final round.

In news that would reverberate throughout the empire for years to come, the cost of this terrible day in British military annals would be 268 killed and 828 wounded, a stunning 50 percent.

BOB MCDONALD

PRIVATE COLLECTION

Loyalist Highlander, Moore's Creek.

MR. AND MRS. RICHARD ULBRICH

*Continental Independent
Rifle Corps, 1776.*

ARTIST COMMENTS

Since militia were involved in this battle, I was free to use models of all age groups, character types, and builds. From farmers to shopkeepers, all rallied that day in 1775 to defend their rights. I tried to convey this image by deliberately placing the younger men and boys next to more senior types for contrast. One of the models was my sixteen-year-old nephew, Marc, and another was noted arms collector Richard Ulbrich, who lives nearby. Dick, who has an incredible collection of original colonial firearms, brought some period New England fowling pieces for him and Marc to pose with. There is even a possibility that one or both of these guns may have been used in the real battle. A dirt pile in my backyard served as the freshly constructed redoubt. Rather than paint the British assault, I wanted to concentrate on the patriots and their emotions as they viewed the oncoming splendor and might of the approaching British regulars. What thoughts could have been going through their minds as they faced the finest troops in the world?

GEORGE WASHINGTON, NEW YORK CAMPAIGN OF 1776

Early November's leaden sky looming above the line of march aptly sets the tone for this portrait of Gen. George Washington in 1776. At forty-four and easily excelling in both strength and stamina men on his staff half his age, he certainly had been superbly endowed to meet the physical demands of the campaign. The army's performance record of the prior ten weeks, though, in ranging from merely disappointing to near disastrous, hinted to some of his countrymen that qualities of "His Excellency" other than physical might need be taken up for debate, whether in Congress or tavern assembled. A man as consistently realistic as attendant to his public reputation, he was enabled to note several apparently eager contenders for his job.

As the ides of November neared in upper Westchester, it was good that neither Washington nor any fellow revolutionary was now prescient, since fortunes that had been bleak were about to become black. In merely a week's time, after daringly dividing the army at Peekskill and taking less than half of it across the Hudson, the general would witness from across the river the heartbreaking capture of the fort on the upper west side of Manhattan that bore his name, and then begin the long, grueling retreat across Jersey toward the hoped-for sanctuary of the Delaware River. By the time the command was safely crossed to Pennsylvania, its numbers qualified as little more than a remnant, and the early snows began to fall. As the final week of 1776 neared, prospects had hit bottom.

If anyone who knew Washington planned to wager against him, though, he neither truly understood the man nor should have dabbled in gaming. For among the taproots of the general's character, none anchored more deeply than duty, daring, and determination. Their combination enabled during the next ten days the dual masterpieces of Trenton and Princeton. While others might, never again would Washington doubt his own capacity. Ever after 1776, he was determination incarnate; he was the Revolution.

BOB MCDONALD

3rd New Jersey Regiment (Jersey Blues), 1776.

BRUCE B. HERMAN

Fusilier, Hesse Cassel Regiment Erb Prinz, 1776.

Hessian Fusilier cap of the Regiment Von Knyphausen,
captured at Trenton. TROIANI COLLECTION

THE ONEIDAS AT THE BATTLE OF ORISKANY, AUGUST 6, 1777

The ambush was perfectly placed: The dirt road snaked down to a ravine before rising again and coming to yet another ravine. It was closely hemmed in by standing hemlocks and other trees, broken at one point by a large blow down from a prior tornado. On the heights above the second ravine, the light infantry of the Royal Regiment of New York were placed to block the advance guard of the patriot militia. Supporting the green-coated Loyalists was a small detachment of Hesse-Hanau Jaegers, also in green. On the high ground commanding one side of the road between the two ravines, their Native American allies were carefully concealed in anticipation of the pending assault on the main body of the "rebel" column of Americans. Closing the trap in the rear were John Brant and his band of Mohawks.

Some 800 men from the Tryon County militia were strung out in a column extending for about a mile, hampered by the narrow track and a slow-moving baggage train of ox-drawn wagons and carts in their rear. They had set out two days earlier to relieve the patriot garrison at Fort Stanwix. This strategic post was the gateway to the Mohawk Valley, and if it fell, the entire valley would be laid to waste by the invading Crown forces. It was not quite 10 A.M., and the men were only four miles from their ultimate goal. Sixty warriors from the Oneida nation reinforced the militia, but instead of their superior woods skills being used on the flanks and in advance, most of the Oneida warriors marched in a body behind the lead regiment of the militia.

Suddenly, before the supply train had fully crossed the first ravine, a shot rang out from near the center. The trap was sprung, but too soon. In a

ONEIDA INDIAN NATION

Bennington.

Dead militiaman—a pose that didn't make it onto canvas.

matter of seconds, the forest understory was enveloped by clouds of acrid, black-powder smoke from the discharge of rifles, muskets, and fowlers. His leg shattered by the ball that killed his horse, the militia commander, Gen. Nicholas Herkimer, resolutely directed his men. After the initial shock wore off, the militia and Oneida fought back valiantly, taking advantage of the tree cover in the same fashion that their enemy had earlier, often fighting in teams of two, one firing while the other reloaded. The Oneida war captain Tewahangaraghkan fought valiantly at close quarters, wielding a tomahawk while his wife, Senagena (Two Kettles), reloaded his fusil for him. To counter this, the Royal Yorker "light bobs" and Jaegers mounted a brave, but ultimately futile, bayonet charge. After hours of fighting, both sides had

3rd New York Regiment, 1777.

34th Regiment of Foot, 1777.

suffered heavy casualties and were exhausted, with ammunition running low. Finally, almost as if by mutual consent, the daylong battle ended with the attackers withdrawing back to their camps. Though the invading army had prevented the relief of the fort, ultimately the events of the day led to the abandonment of the siege and the invaders' subsequent retreat.

JAMES L. KOCHAN

ARTIST COMMENTS

This large 50-by-80-inch oil on canvas was commissioned by the Oneida Indian Nation to commemorate the brave service of Chief Honyery Tewahangaraghkan; his wife, Senagena; and a band of warriors of that tribe fighting with the patriots in the bloody battle. It is always especially gratifying for me

to be able to spotlight some of the unsung heroes of American history.

At the time of this painting, Jim Kochan had just purchased an original Hanau Jaeger rifle, so its details were incorporated into the hands of this cautious Jaeger at the very last minute. Many times, fresh information arrives at the eleventh hour and repainting must be done. Although the viewer's eye quickly goes to the figures, most of the endless hours spent on this work involved painting the woodlands. It can easily take an hour to paint a few ferns alone. I used heavy underpainting on the tree bark followed by washes of thin color to replicate the gnarled texture of the wood. I wanted to achieve the effect of deep old woodlands, so I kept the foreground darker while throwing some light into the background areas.

BREYMANN'S REDOUBT

In the late spring of 1777, with the American Revolution still in the balance, Gen. John Burgoyne began his march south toward Albany, New York, with an army of more than 9,000 Crown forces. They fought actions at Fort Ticonderoga and Mount Independence, Hubbardton, Fort Ann, and Bennington (Walloomsac), New York. By mid September, Burgoyne had crossed to the west side of the Hudson River and was moving south toward new American fortified positions at Bemis Heights. Elements of the American army, by then under Gen. Horatio Gates, halted Burgoyne's army in the first battle of Saratoga on September 19, 1777.

Within days of this engagement, Burgoyne set his army to work on a series of field fortifications and waited for Gates's next move. Finally, on October 7, he launched a reconnaissance in force of more than 1,700 soldiers against the left flank of the American fortifications. Advancing slightly less than a mile, they deployed in a line of battle across two fields and woods near the Barber Farm. American forces then attacked and drove the entire force back into the Balcarre's Redoubt on the right flank of Burgoyne's fortified lines. Although he had been relieved of command by Gates, Maj. Gen. Benedict Arnold rode on the field of battle, where he encouraged the men and led advance after advance with bravery and tactical leadership.

After failing to breach the Balcarre's Redoubt, Arnold galloped north to join American forces forming to assault the Breymann Redoubt and two fortified cabins in the gap between the redoubts. These undermanned fortified cabins were captured and thus uncovered the left of the Breymann Redoubt. As the bulk of Learned's Brigade and Morgan's Light Corps advanced against the front of the redoubt, Arnold stormed into the Germans' rear and left flank with part of Lt. Col. John Brooks's Massachusetts Continental Regiment and a collection of fifteen to twenty riflemen. A Brunswick grenadier platoon shot him, killing his horse and wounding him in the leg. As Brunswick colonel Heinrich Breymann fell, resistance collapsed. With the fall of the Breymann Redoubt,

2nd Light Continental Dragoons.

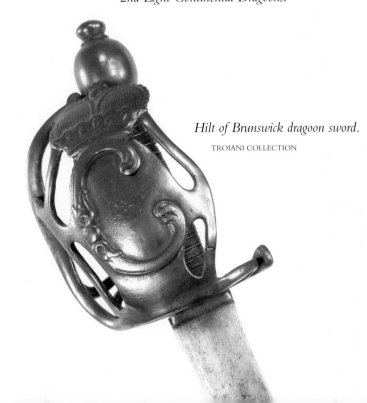

Hilt of Brunswick dragoon sword.

almost all of Burgoyne's positions were exposed and became untenable. The Americans had won the second battle of Saratoga, and by October 17, they had forced Burgoyne's army to surrender.

ANTHONY W. TOMMEL

ARTIST COMMENTS

The great battles of the Revolution have never really been painted much by American artists. For reasons unexplained the painters of this country have not chronicled military history as extensively as their European counterparts.

I had done a watercolor version of this scene in the 1970s for the National Park Service, but I always felt it was such an important event that it really needed the full oil painting treatment. Having been interested for many years in the uniforms and equipage of the Brunswick troops, I found

Brunswick Dragoon.

this painting an opportunity to depict them in rich detail based on original artifacts. I posed the officer and sergeant holding original Brunswick pole arms and the privates with original muskets from my collection. A small number of German artifacts remain from this campaign, and these were invaluable in helping me get the details correct. A grenadier cap of the Regiment Von Specht in the Massachusetts State House, a trophy of Bennington, provided detail for the embossing on the cap front.

To give the sky depth, I used a very thin paint surface with no texture. The figures and ground cover were more heavily worked with thick brush strokes, which make the figures pop forward. The emblems on the grenadiers' caps each took more than two hours to paint, and the drum two days.

Breymann's Redoubt sketched in on the gesso panel.

Hessian officer's partizan with cipher of Frederick Landgraf II.
TROIANI COLLECTION

Sergeant Grenadier Regiment von Rall, Trenton, 1776.   BRUCE B. HERMAN

MOLLY PITCHER AT MONMOUTH

In writing his memoirs of Continental army service, Joseph Plumb Martin recalled an incident at the battle of Monmouth, New Jersey, on June 28, 1778:

> A woman whose husband belonged to the artillery . . . attended with her husband at the piece the whole time. While in the act of reaching a cartridge and having one of her feet as far before the other as she could step, a cannon shot from the enemy passed directly between her legs without doing any more damage than carrying away all the lower part of her petticoat. Looking at it with apparent unconcern, she . . . continued with her work.

In her mid twenties and plain in appearance, Mary Hays was compact and strong. More than a decade of earning a wage through domestic service had accustomed her body to daily labor and heightened her sense of responsibility. As a result, when husband William enlisted in Proctor's Pennsylvania Artillery in the spring of 1777, she was a virtually ideal candidate to join the ranks of the army wives and camp followers.

The traditional recounting of events at Monmouth has Mary repeatedly toting water to the gun crew until William fell from the heat of that torrid afternoon or from a wound. Although this earned her the nickname of Molly Pitcher, she more likely used a wooden bucket. Stepping up to the vacancy, she passed ammunition and also may have loaded and rammed the piece. Accounts of her determined and tenacious service spread throughout the army in a matter of days as the Continentals celebrated their signal victory. Thereafter, she was often addressed as Sergeant, Captain, or even Major Molly.

As a widow in 1822, Molly became one of only three women granted pensions for services performed during the Revolution. When she died at age seventy-nine a decade later, the local militia turned out to march in her funeral procession.

BOB MCDONALD

Original British common light 3-pound gun from my collection. The pog is modern.

4th Continental Light Dragoons.

Private Lewis's Troop, 3rd Continental Light Dragoons, 1777–78.

NATIONAL PARK SERVICE

Beltplate of the 33rd Regiment of Foot found near Saratoga. TROIANI COLLECTION

ARTIST COMMENTS

I could not locate an original French light 4-pound gun to use as a prop for this painting. The only available solution was to use as a stand-in the original 3-pound British common light gun from my collection. I converted it on canvas. Although preferring to use the real article, in this case that wasn't an option.

Rebecca Fifield from the costume department of the Metropolitan Museum of Art in New York posed as Molly wearing splendid reconstructed period garments. To help create the sense of the heat of the original battle, I used a sprayer bottle and garden hose to liberally apply a heavy mist to the models. Dripping wet, they glistened in the bright sunlight. When painting artillery in action, it is vital to remember what a truly filthy job it is to deal with black powder. Faces, hands, and clothing are soon blackened, as are the muzzle of the guns from the discharges. As the powder on the muzzles cool, it becomes bluish gray.

Dragoon, Lee's Legion, 1779.

Queen's Ranger,
Light Infantry.

HERMAN BENNINGHOFF

33rd Regiment of Foot,
1780.

Cartridge-box badge of the
Light Company of the British
63rd Regiment of Foot.

TROIANI COLLECTION

PRIVATE COLLECTION

COWPENS

On the clear, cold morning of January 17, 1781, Gen. Daniel Morgan's small detached command of 2,000 men was organizing near the cattle herders' station known locally as Hannah's Cowpens. Just a few hundred yards separated its two lines from the despised scourge of South Carolina, Lt. Col. Banastre Tarleton, in command of 1,200 British regulars and Loyalists. Beginning their advance at 7 A.M., red-coat light infantry and Tarleton's own British Legion were closely followed by the main body of the 7th Fusiliers, two 3-pounder guns, and the 71st Regiment of Foot. Col. Andrew Pickens's front line of 1,000 American militiamen delayed their fire until the enemy was only 150 yards away, then delivered two enviable volleys, many of the shooters taking special aim at the recognizably uniformed British officers. Then they faced about and marched to the rear. It was only after this withdrawing force had cleared the central corridor of the field that most of the redcoats got their first glimpse of the second American line, composed of veteran Maryland and Delaware Continentals.

The ensuing quarter-hour firefight was cut short when a misinterpreted order resulted in the virtual entirety of the Continentals about-facing and marching, in near perfect order, rearward. Interpreting this over-optimistically, Tarleton's force plunged ahead impetuously, losing order and control. As Morgan was selecting a new position at which the Continentals could concentrate, he received a message from their commander, Lt. Col. John Eager Howard: "They are coming on like a mob. Give them a fire and I will charge." In response, a composite of Continentals and militia quickly formed a new line. Firing from a mere 100 feet away, their volley was devastating. The British line exploded in car-

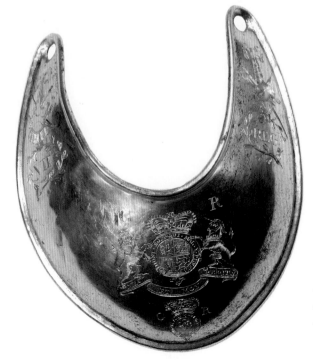

British officer's gilt gorget of the 7th Regiment of Foot.

TROIANI COLLECTION

Private, 17th Light Dragoons, 1780.

nage and stunned shock. The redcoats and loyalists struggled to regain some order. While Howard's Continentals formed in the center, Morgan and Pickens swung the militia force around the enemy's left flank, and Col. William Washington's cavalry flanked them on the right. Double envelopment! In the center, the Delaware and Maryland boys leveled bayonets and charged.

In this scene of the ensuing clash, the 7th Fusiliers were suffering the ultimate loss on a field of battle—that of their colors. While the mounted Lieutenant Colonel Howard swung down on a member of the color guard who valiantly, but futilely, continued to resist, a Continental grasped the regimental standard. Behind them, the Royal standard was but a moment away from capture.

Battle of Cowpens.

His Majesty's loss of men at Cowpens nearly strains credulity. Morgan's total force had sustained only two dozen killed and approximately 100 wounded, but 200 of Tarleton's men were dead on the field or had suffered mortal wounds, and upward of 700 prisoners had been taken, nearly 200 of whom were wounded. In about one hour's time, Tarleton had lost 75 percent of his force, a stunning loss approaching a quarter of Lord Cornwallis's southern army. Nine months later, the true extent of that cost would be realized at York-town.

BOB MCDONALD

Gaskin's Virginia Battalion.

French Saintonge Regiment of Infantry.

ARTIST COMMENTS

I was fortunate to consult with Larry Babbits, the consummate expert on the battle and author of *Devil of a Whipping*, and he provided many important facts and insights. As always, Jim Kochan and I worked closely on the uniforms and equipment. Jim happened to be in the area of the battlefield on the anniversary and braved the freezing cold to photograph the area at the crack of dawn. Being there on the anniversary of the battle gave me a real feel for the lighting.

I had both silk flags of the Royal Fusiliers reproduced to serve as models for the painting, but as things turned out, they wound up barely seen in the background. I hope they will serve me another day.

Washington and Rochambeau at Yorktown, 1781.

Officer, Maryland Line, 1780–81.

Cornwallis at Yorktown, 1781.

HERMAN BENNINGHOFF

The New Republic and Western Expansion, 1784–1859

NORTH POINT

ARTIST COMMENTS

This painting of the 1814 battle outside Baltimore was commissioned by the U.S. Army National Guard Bureau in the early 1980s and represents as tight a situation as an artist can get into. Although great to work with, the National Guard allowed only six to nine months for the painting to be researched and completed. That's not much time, but well within the realm of possibility, if the research is not difficult to come by. The problem was, the Guard required a pencil sketch first. That, too, is a reasonable request, but it often took six months to be approved. All the while, the contract clock was still ticking, and by the time I was granted the go-ahead, only a month or two remained to pose and paint the picture. On commission work, I try to have at least a year or two for delivery.

Private, Scott's Brigade (9th, 11th, and 25th U.S. Infantry), Spring–Summer 1814.

Private, Light Company, 104th (New Brunswick) Regiment of Foot, Summer 1814.

Soldier, 4th United States Infantry, 1811.

Ensign and Private, 25th U.S. Infantry, Fall 1813–Spring 1814.

Officer's coatee of the 37th Regiment of Foot, circa 1812–15.
MOIANI COLLECTION

U.S. Marine Corps Drum, 1840.
TROIANI COLLECTION

The artist's 1812 reproduction caps for use with models.

Infantry officer's bell-crown shako.
TROIANI COLLECTION

Trooper, 1st Regiment of U.S. Dragoons, 1846–47.

U.S. pattern of 1813 shako with cords.

Sergeant, U.S. Marines, 1828.

"The Recall," U.S. Dragoons, 1850s.

The Civil War, 1861–1865

New York's Bravest

No regiment entered the first battle of Bull Run with such high expectations of glory than the 11th New York, the Fire Zouaves. Members of Manhattan's volunteer fire department and largely of Irish descent, the Zouaves were famed for their physical prowess and reckless courage. They had gone to war led by charismatic young Col. Elmer Ellsworth, whose death at the hands of a Virginia innkeeper fired the red-shirted Zouaves with a desire for vengeance. But the firemen, now under the command of Col. Noah Farnham, found the holocaust of battle more daunting than even the most perilous conflagration.

When Capt. James Ricketts's and Capt. Charles Griffin's batteries were deployed atop Henry Hill to pave the way for what seemed certain Union victory, the 11th New York was ordered to support the artillerists. But the Confederates rallied and lashed out at the exposed position. The Zouave line was staggered by enemy volleys, and as several companies fell back, they were charged by Col. Jeb Stuart's 1st Virginia Cavalry. Southern infantry surged forward, overrunning the batteries, and with Colonel Farnham wounded, the 11th ceased to function as a cohesive entity. Even so, knots of red-shirted Zouaves joined newly arrived Federal units who desperately sought to recapture the guns on Henry Hill.

Col. Michael Corcoran's 69th New York State Militia was among the regiments whose time had come to test their mettle on the bullet-swept hillside. Theirs was a patriotism doubly strong, for their ranks were composed of Irish-Americans, and alongside the Stars and Stripes, the 69th carried the green banner of Ireland—the symbol of the freedom they hoped to win for the Emerald Isle. The flag's inscription symbolized their defiant pride, commemorating the controversial events of the previous October, when Corcoran had refused to parade his regiment before the visiting Prince of Wales.

Presentation of New York's Bravest print to the New York Fire Department.

WILLIAM RODEN

Col. William T. Sherman fed the regiments of his brigade into the cataclysm piecemeal. With the 13th New York engaged north of the shell-splintered Henry House, the 2nd Wisconsin advanced from the sunken Sudley Road, only to be thrown into disorder. The 79th New York Highlanders were next and shared a similar fate—their commander, Col. James Cameron, was among the slain. "At last the order came for the 69th to try and do what others had failed in," one Irishman recalled; "we were like sheep sent to the slaughter." With the 69th went two dozen Fire Zouaves under the command of Capt. John Wildey, the strapping foreman of Manhattan's Engine Company 11, known as "Oceanus."

Exhausted by a forced march in the sweltering heat, the Irishmen nonetheless went bravely into the fray. Like many soldiers of both armies, they stripped for battle, tossing aside jackets and all but their weapons, cartridge boxes, and canteens. Some men went in bare-chested, like prizefighters ready for a knockdown brawl. As the line went cheering up the hill, Capt. Thomas Francis Meagher, also acting major—the cele-

Company K, 69th New York State Militia.

MICHAEL FLANAGAN

1st North Carolina Cavalry, 1861.

6th Regiment Massachusetts
Volunteer Militia, 1861.

brated Irish patriot and orator whose Irish Zouaves served as the 69th's Color Company—was thrown to the ground when his horse was cut down by a cannonball. Meagher got to his feet and, flourishing his sword at the green banner borne by Color Sgt. John Murphy, shouted, "Boys! Look at that flag! Remember Ireland and Fontenoy!" The reference to the French victory of 1745 over an English army, won in large part because of the gallantry of Irish troops, inspirited the 69th, but the assault faltered before the stalwart resistance of the Hampton Legion and other Southern units.

Bolstered by reinforcements, the Confederates counterattacked amidst the shambles of the disabled batteries, and when the Federals recoiled, Murphy found himself in a desperate struggle to save his green banner from capture. Wounded in the thigh, Murphy was helpless to fend off his foes. It was at that moment that Capt. Jack Wildey, revolver in hand, led a determined group of Zouaves and men of the 69th to the rescue. Wildey gunned down the Confederate who had seized the flag, then shot another assailant. The captain later compared the melee to "an old-time firemen's fight," when rival companies used to battle for the honor of quenching a blaze. An admiring 69th soldier thought Wildey's Zouaves "fought like devils."

BRIAN POHANKA AND KEITH KNOKE

Up Alabamians.

ARTIST COMMENTS

This painting required making sense out of highly varied, conflicting, and overblown accounts of the same episode. Additionally, both sides were dressed in nearly identical uniforms. Many soldiers had removed their coats and fought in shirtsleeves, further confusing the process of determining who was on which side—a problem for both the period combatants and the modern artist. The location of this event remarkably still looks about the same as it did on the day of the battle, thanks to the efforts of the National Park Service.

*11th Virginia Infantry, Company E
(The Lynchburg Rifles), July 1861.*

First Regiment South Carolina Rifles, 1861.

FIRST AT MANASSAS

Numbering but 300 strong, the 1st Virginia Cavalry spent the morning of July 21, 1861, scouting the lower fords of Bull Run, all the while impatiently listening to the sounds of battle a little more than a mile to the north. The troopers did not have long to wait before they were called on to help their vastly outnumbered comrades fighting in and around the Edgar Matthew and Judith Henry farms. On reaching the southern slopes of Henry House Hill, Col. Jeb Stuart received orders from Brig. Gen. Thomas J. Jackson to project his flanks. Splitting his command in two, Colonel Stuart directed Maj. Robert Swan to take three companies to Jackson's right flank while he led the other three to Jackson's hard-pressed left.

Marching to the same destination as Stuart and his troopers, but from the opposite direction, were Union soldiers in Col. Samuel P. Heintzelman's division. Near the vanguard of this force was the 11th New York Infantry, Ellsworth's Fire Zouaves, who were eager to live up to a reputation that had grown to almost mythical proportions. Their march had brought them to the foot of Henry House Hill. To their front and near the top of the hill were two Union artillery batteries, which were then heavily engaged with Confederate artillery and infantry. Preoccupied with the events occurring to their front, they did not give much thought to their unprotected right flank.

Having just arrived on the Confederate left and opposite the New Yorkers' exposed right flank, Colonel Stuart wasted little time in assessing the situation. Sensing an opportunity, he ordered the bugler to sound a charge. "Setting up a terrible yell," wrote a Virginian, "we charged upon them, our gallant Colonel leading the way." Aware now of this new threat, the Fire Zouaves reacted quickly, with portions re-forming to meet the onslaught. "They formed hastily into line," wrote one fireman, "kneeling, semi-kneeling, and standing," as they quickly prepared to fire. The quick response of the New Yorkers was not lost on the Virginians. Recalling the event, one trooper wrote, "Half the distance was passed before they saw the avalanche coming upon them, but then they came to a front face, a long line of bright muskets were leveled, a sheet of red flame gleamed and we could see no more." Down in a tumbling mass of dust, horses, and riders went the lead troopers. Undaunted, the troopers continued their charge, each grasping his weapon of choice, be it a revolver, saber, or carbine, striking the firemen's hastily formed line and scattering them "like chaff before the wind."

Colonel Stuart and the troopers of the 1st Virginia cavalry had succeeded in helping to check the Union advance. Although the day was far from over for both units, the tide was beginning to sway in favor of the Confederate forces. In a few short hours, the once confident men of the Union army, who only a few days earlier were shouting, "On to Richmond!" found themselves in a less than orderly retreat back to Washington.

KEITH KNOKE

ARTIST COMMENTS

One of the reasons I stopped using mounted models for certain action sequences was because of an incident when sculptor Ron Tunison was posing for me. We were doing some scenes where Ron, fully uniformed and equipped, would ride directly at me at a full gallop while I shot pictures. As he sped toward me, he would take a swing at me with his saber. Trying to shoot pictures and not get run over was becoming a problem. Seeing a stake lying nearby, I planted it in the ground and told Ron to dash toward it and swipe at it with his saber. He took off, but just as the horse reached the mark, it bucked and Ron went flying. Remarkably, while in midair, he managed to drop his saber and pitch off the carbine. Fortunately he came through with little injury. It happened that the stake was the type used in the electric fencing at the stable, so the horse did not want to get near it.

Flag historian Steve Hill made a copy of the unique Fire Zouave flag to serve as a model for this painting, and several red firemen's shirts were made up for those modeling Zouaves. I spent time researching appropriate tattoos for the bare arms of the Zouaves, as well as other distinctive items, such as the firemen's badges and belts. It was fortunate that only the flank companies of the 11th had Model 1855 rifles with saber bayonets, as I had just a single example in my collection.

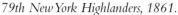

79th New York Highlanders, 1861.

DICK AND M. E. CLOW

Lance Corporal, Irish Jasper Greens,
Fall 1861.

DRIVE THEM TO WASHINGTON

BOOTH MUSEUM OF WESTERN ART, CARTERSVILLE, GEORGIA

Composed of the 2nd, 4th, 5th, 27th, and 33rd Virginia Infantry Regiments, the 1st Brigade of the Army of the Shenandoah began its long and storied history on the plains of Manassas in July 1861. Commanded by Brig. Gen. Thomas J. Jackson, the brigade left Winchester, Virginia, on the afternoon of July 18, 1861, arriving at Manassas Junction in the predawn hours of Saturday, July 20. The men settled in along the banks of Bull Run for a well-deserved rest and were no doubt pondering what the next day would bring.

Early the next morning, the brigade awoke to the sound cannon fire. After a hastily prepared breakfast, the Virginians took up their line of march, first north and then south as the Confederates tried to discern Union general Irvin McDow-

ell's true intentions. The crossing of two Union divisions at Sudley Ford, located beyond the Confederate left flank, made McDowell's plans evident. With Col. James F. Preston's 4th Virginia infantry taking the lead, the brigade counter-marched, much of it at double-quick time, heading north to meet the Union threat. Arriving footsore and thirsty, the men of the brigade reached the slopes of Henry Hill around noon.

General Jackson, quickly assessing the situation, placed his brigade near the hill's southeast edge. Forming the extreme right of the brigade was the 5th Virginia. To its left was the 4th and 27th Virginia Regiments, the latter in position imme-diately behind the former. To their left formed the 2nd Vir-ginia, and anchoring the brigade's left flank was the undersize

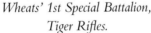

GREENSBORO HISTORY MUSEUM

Wheats' 1st Special Battalion,
Tiger Rifles.

DAVID R. RANKIN JR.

Private, Company I, 4th Virginia Infantry
(The Liberty Hall Volunteers).

33rd Virginia. To further bolster the position, General Jackson placed a formidable line of thirteen cannons in front of his infantry brigade. With the position of the infantry and artillery now settled, the men of the 1st Brigade had little to do but wait and endure the intense heat and incessant Union artillery fire.

Although meant as counter battery fire, many of the Union artillery rounds overshot their Confederate counterparts and took effect on Jackson's infantry. "Whilst laying upon the ground," recalled one junior officer, "any number of shot and shell passed within a few feet of me, or may have been but a few inches. I could not see them, could hear the whizzing sound and felt the movement of the air. One passed so near as to cause the skirt of my havelock to fly up, raised

the hair on the head of the man immediately behind me and exploded about 20 feet distant." Many soldiers of the brigade were not so lucky, however. "Whilst lying there," wrote one Virginian, "a fatal shell burst in the midst of our company, killed three of our boys and wounded another. . . . We lay in that awful place for at least two hours, during which time the suspense was of the most agonizing character."

The Federal advance on Henry Hill would soon bring an end to the Virginians' anxious wait. Federal commanders sent regiment after regiment up the slopes of Henry Hill, but they were sent tumbling back by the combined effects of Confederate artillery and musketry. Nonetheless, the seemingly endless supply of Federal troops caused General Jackson to call for the use of bayonets. Riding to the left of the 4th Virginia, the

*De Kalb Zouaves, 41st New York
Volunteer Infantry, 1861.*

TIM OSTERHELD

4th Virginia Cavalry (Black Horse Troop), 1861.   DON THARPE

general ordered the men of the 4th and 27th Virginia to stand up and "charge and drive them to Washington!" No longer just spectators, the two regiments surged forward, driving the Federal infantry before them and ultimately capturing some of the cannons that had bombarded them only moments before. With the aid of newly arriving Confederate reinforcements, the Virginians succeeded in pushing the Federal infantry off of Henry Hill, setting the stage for an overwhelming Confederate victory on the plains of Manassas.

KEITH KNOKE

ARTIST COMMENTS

I've always had an issue with contemporary renderings of "Old Jack" at First Manassas, particularly his floppy cap. Jack-son's appearance on the battlefield that day is clearly described in a well-known and readily available reprinted book, in which Lt. W. M. Miller Owen of the Washington Artillery gave this splendid account: "He had been slightly wounded in the hand, and had it bound up in his handkerchief. He was a very quiet plain-looking man dressed in a blue military coat, and wore the shoulder straps of a colonel in the United States army. His cap was of the old army pattern, in vogue during the Mexican war—blue cloth, flat on top." This is the U.S. pattern of 1839 forage cap, a style still worn during the 1860s by civilian and military, although gradually falling out of favor. I have added a Virginia "Old English" wreath to the front, as required by state regulations of the time.

First Battle Flags

The morning of November 28, 1861, opened with clear skies—at least clearer than the cold, gray overcast of the preceding five days. A decision was made: Today would begin the distribution (originally planned for the twenty-fourth) of the new battle flags. The three brigades of Longstreet's 2nd Division would be the first to receive the honor. At 10:30 A.M., these brigades were drawn up into an open-ended hollow square. At the open end were the general officers of the Confederate Army of the Potomac: Gen. Joseph Johnston in command; his two corps commanders, Gen. P. G. T. Beauregard and Gen. Gustavus Smith; and the division commanders, James Longstreet and Earl Van Dorn, the latter with his recently presented personal battle flag. Along with their staffs, they were drawn up with the new battle flags to be presented.

The new battle flag that was about to be presented was the brainchild of General Beauregard. At the battle of Manassas four months earlier, Beauregard's pensive nervousness had been put to the test over the identities of units whose Confedeate Stars and Bars so resembled the Union's Stars and Stripes that he could not tell if they were friend or foe. In early September, in an attempt to alleviate this problem, Beauregard had proposed that the Confederate forces carry a special distinctive flag that could not be mistaken for the flag of the old Union.

In Richmond, Lt. C. McRae Selph cleared the shelves of the dry goods merchants of all suitable commercial dress silk. He then set several ladies' sewing circles, eventually numbering seventy-five women, to work fabricating flags from the material he had purchased. By October 21, a sample was ready, and with its approval by Beauregard, efforts were redoubled to complete the rest. According to Selph, by mid November, 120 flags had been prepared and delivered to Centerville, where the winter camps of the Confederate Army of the Potomac were concentrated.

The ceremonies began on the twenty-eighth with an address read by Beauregard's assistant adjutant general, Thomas Jordan. Then the dismounted colonels of the twelve regiments present successively stepped forward from the line drawn up in front of the generals and their staffs, and each received from the hands of General Beauregard one of the battle flags.

All moved smoothly until Col. Robert E. Withers, commanding officer of the 18th Virginia Infantry, stepped forward. As scarlet silk had been an item of great demand for dresses, Lieutenant Selph had been forced to purchase silk in shades of "red of all tints—magenta, solfernio, pink, etc." Colonel Withers was presented with one of those made from

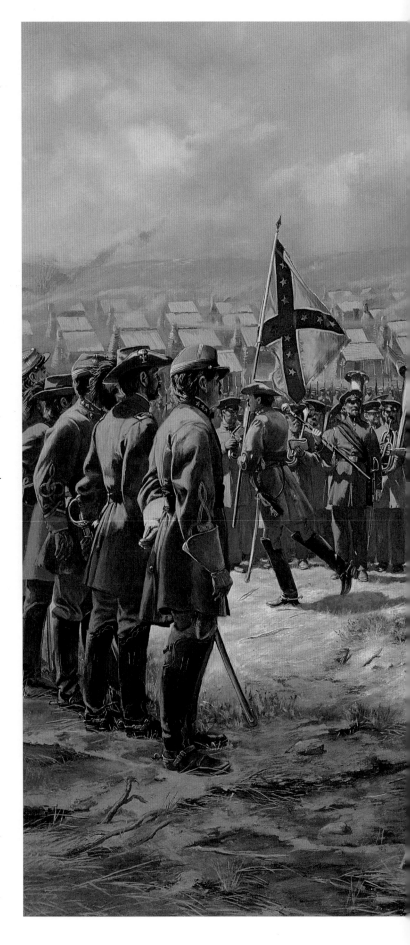

the pink silk. When General Beauregard presented it, Withers said, after his acceptance thanks, the comment, "I have but one objection to it; its color is indicative of fear, and looks too much like a flag of truce." Beauregard hesitated but briefly before responding: "Dye it red sir! Dye it in blood sir!" Withers quickly acknowledged, "It shall be sir. It shall be, in the blood of the enemy, General!" Beauregard retorted, "In your own, sir, if necessary."

The ceremonies concluded with each regiment saluting its new color, followed by a grand view of all the regiments present, during which the bands played patriotic airs. Over the next two years, the Southern Cross battle flags spread to nearly all the military units of the Confederacy, and they were bathed in both blood and glory.

HOWARD M. MADAUS

ARTIST COMMENTS

I was surprised to receive some criticism about the color of the battle flags in this painting. Some people thought they looked washed out, as they did not fit into the preconceived notion of what a "real" Confederate battle flag should be. Even after constant explaining, I am fairly certain that some still cannot bring themselves to accept the fact that the Confederate army used pink battle flags. To get the flying flags just right, I had flag expert Steven Hill make me an example of each type, in both the off-white and pink silk.

DAVID R. RANKIN JR.

12th Tennessee Regiment, C.S.A.

14th Mississippi Infantry, C.S.A.

Men of Arkansas

"Men of Arkansas, you boast of using cold steel, don't waste your ammunition. I will lead you." With these words, Gen. Albert Sidney Johnston led his routed division into a successful counterattack, one in which he was mortally wounded. There has been much debate about Johnston's ability as an army commander, but his reputation from before the war was impressive and led Jefferson Davis to say of him, "I hoped and expected that I had others who would prove generals, but I knew I had one, and that was Sidney Johnston." Even more powerful were the words of Johnston's adversary that April day in 1862, Ulysses S. Grant, who said that "he expected him to prove the most formidable man that the Confederacy could produce."

Johnston's reputation had suffered in the early days of 1862 as Federal armies crashed through his department, driving his forces from Kentucky through Tennessee and into northern Mississippi. He gathered his forces around Corinth and was joined by reinforcements from the Gulf coast and other points. Seeing that he had one last chance to change his luck when Federal forces halted their advance and camped along the Tennessee River at Pittsburg Landing, Johnston quickly made plans for an attack and marched his army northward. This resulted in the Battle of Shiloh. The general was renewed and showed great energy as he dashed along his lines on April 6, leading his army as a captain would lead his company. Johnston knew how to lead volunteers in battle. He spoke encouragement to them, rallied them personally when they faltered, and made his commanding figure visible, showing them that he shared the dangers with them.

At one point during the day, he chastised a young soldier for looting, but on seeing the dejection on the soldier's face, Johnston took a tin cup as his share of the spoils. He bran-

Gutta Percha rubberized rain hat taken from the body of a dead Confederate soldier after the battle of Corinth.

TROIANI COLLECTION

Private, 1st Arkansas Mounted Rifles,   DAVID R. RANKIN JR.
Company D, 1861.

WILLIAM RODEN

19th Tennessee Infantry, C.S.A.

dished that cup several times during the day, including when he addressed and led the 9th Arkansas into battle. He fell a short time later, at a moment when it seemed that victory was certain. With his death, there was a lapse in iniative as the command of the army was passed along to Gen. P. G. T. Beauregard. The Federal army was reinforced during the night, and the battle was lost.

In the aftermath, Johnston's reputation was saved by his death on the field of battle, and his name was propelled into the realm of legend. The *Southern Illustrated News* wrote that Johnston "fell where heroes love to fall—in the arms of victory upon the battlefield." In death, he found redemption.

LEE WHITE

34th Ohio Volunteer Infantry, Piatt's Zouaves.

Rifle Company, 56th New York Volunteer Infantry (10th Legion), 1862.

ARTIST COMMENTS

I have never understood why no artist had chosen to paint this inspiring scene. Early war scenes such as this one allow me to show a greater variety of uniforms and accoutrements. I am particularly fond of battle shirts but rarely have an opportunity to place any in a painting. The Arkansas troops were armed with a huge conglomeration of outmoded weapons, including double-barrel shotguns, flintlock muskets, Hall breech-loading rifles, and, best of all, monstrously large

Bowie knives. I have a good assortment of these weapons in my collection, and the models were posed brandishing the original items. Bowies were immensely popular at the outbreak of the war, with some huge Confederate specimens being, in reality, short swords. The opportunity to use them in action rarely occurred, and soon they became unwieldy encumbrances for soldiers on the march. By the middle of 1862, few were seen among veteran troops.

THE RED DEVILS

In the year since they had been rallied to the colors by wealthy Manhattan businessman Abram Duryea, now a brigadier general, the 5th New York Zouaves had taken part in only one real engagement. That June 1861 clash at Big Bethel had won the flashy unit the sobriquet Red Devils, and the subsequent months of garrison duty in occupied Baltimore had seen West Pointer G. K. Warren bring their drill and discipline on par with that of the Regular army. The Zouaves were anxious to prove themselves, and on June 27, 1862, they would get their chance.

Warren's 10th New York was screened by a copse of pine trees, but the 5th New York remained vulnerable in an open field, and at Lieutenant Colonel Duryea's urging, Warren ordered them to fall back to the partial shelter afforded by a sunken roadbed.

Finally the enemy made his appearance, Gen. Maxcy Gregg's South Carolina brigade deploying from the facing woodline, the 1st South Carolina Orr's Rifles in the vanguard. At Warren's signal, Duryea ordered the red legs into line of battle. The Zouaves went forward with a cheer, scrambling up the muddy embankment and jogging into place, then sweeping across the field at a half-left wheel to close with the South Carolinians.

As the first bullets began to tear through the ranks, the charge briefly lost momentum. Gouverneur Warren spurred his gray horse to the color company, K, and yelled, "Advance the colors! Advance the colors! Charge!"

Some opponents crossed bayonets before Orr's Rifles gave way. "The enemy was driven from the field in confusion," Duryea reported, "and the survivors nearly annihilated by our fire." One South Carolinian called the Zouaves' onslaught "the most desperate charge I ever witnessed in the war." "The Zouaves, on our left front, behaved splendidly," a regular of the 12th U.S. noted. "There was no flinching, no dropping to the rear. They stood like heroes to their work, under a murderous fire."

When Color Sgt. Francis Spelman collapsed with heat stroke, the state banner was raised by Company D's Sgt. John H. Berrian, whose brother had been slain moments before. Anguished and enraged, Berrian carried the regimental flag thirty paces in advance of the flaming battle line, planted the staff in the ground, and shook his fist at his Rebel foes. Inspired by Berrian's gesture, Sgt. Andrew B. Allison joined him with the national colors. At first Duryea

Berdan's Sharpshooters.

and the acting field officer, Capt. Cleveland Winslow, shouted at the two men to come back. Instead, the balance of the regiment gave a terrible yell and, as Davenport wrote, "rushed like demons for the wood with the bayonet." But the South Carolinians held firm, and the Union charge dissolved in a murderous fire. The Zouaves' color guard was decimated.

At last a regiment of Pennsylvanians came to their relief, and Duryea pulled his decimated companies out of the line. But before marching them rearward, he ordered them to halt and called them to attention. As Confederate shells exploded overhead, Duryea had his men count off and realign their ranks. Only then did he resume the retreat.

The battle of Gaines's Mill made it clear to friend and foe alike that the Duryea Zouaves were more than a colorful ornament on the parade ground. Of the 450 men with which the unit had entered the fray, 162 had fallen.

BRIAN POHANKA

Louisiana Zouave Battalion, Coppen's Zouaves, 1861.

ARTIST COMMENTS

Zouaves have always been among my favorite subjects, and my old friend, the late scholar Brian Pohanka, had been prodding me to do the 5th New York Zouaves for a long time. Gaines's Mill was probably their finest hour, so we planned to re-create their bloody fight there. Brian, having devoted years to the study of every minute detail of the 5th, was instrumental in getting this as right as humanly possible. Brian was the epitome of a classic Zouave in appearance, so he was posed for the wounded soldier on the right of the picture. We got pictures of the actual site to capture the tall pine trees and whitish sandy soil of the peninsula.

With Brian's recent untimely passing, having painted him among his beloved 5th New York for generations to see, is a humble tribute from his saddened artist comrade.

My oil and watercolor painting table.

THE SOUTHERN CROSS

The fighting at Glendale on June 30, 1862, during the Seven Days' Battles featured some fierce hand-to-hand combat. The focal points for much of this fighting were the Union artillery batteries lined up across the front of the division of Pennsylvania Reserves.

Lt. Alanson M. Randol's Battery E, 1st United States, with six 12-pounder Napoleons, was one of these batteries. Gen. Cadmus M. Wilcox's Alabama brigade of James Longstreet's large division twice charged this battery, only to be repulsed by canister and rifle fire.

Wilcox's third attempt was more successful. The 11th Alabama charged directly into the fierce fire of the battery, which was defended by a mixed force from the 4th and 7th Pennsylvania Reserves. One young Alabamian laid his hand on a cannon tube and proudly exclaimed that the gun was his. A Pennsylvanian shot the man dead, retorting, "Not just yet!" Reported Gen. George A. McCall: "Bayonet wounds, mortal or slight, were given and received. I saw skulls crushed by the butts of muskets."

Charley McNeil, color-bearer of the 11th Alabama, jumped up on one of the cannons to claim the battery for his regiment, but he was soon shot down and fell beneath the cannon, still clutching his flag. His nephew Billy tried to save him but was slain by charging Yankees, who seized the fallen banner as a trophy. Wilcox's men eventually fell back, but Randal's battery was wrecked, surrounded by dead horses and scores of men in blue and gray. The artillery was captured the next morning after the Union army fell back toward Malvern Hill.

DR. RICHARD SAUERS

ARTIST COMMENTS

Balancing on a 12-pound Napoleon gun was not an easy task, as model Joel Bohy discovered. The only way to get it right was to actually position the dressed model with the flag on a real gun. It took a number of tries to find a dramatic yet stable pose, and Joel thankfully did not fall off.

I had three pairs of canvas leggings reproduced for the models for this picture from one of the few known original sets in my collection. Photographic evidence shows the Pennsylvania Reserves wearing this style, which was heavily issued in early 1862 and occasionally afterward. The famed Iron Brigade also wore this identical pattern. With the models wearing these leggings, I was able to see exactly how the heavy sky blue trousers folded when tucked into the gaiters.

55th New York, Lafayette Guard, 1862.

Private, 18th Massachusetts Infantry, January 1862.

BROTHERS OF IRELAND

JOHN KERR

In the gathering twilight of June 27, 1862, the battle of Gaines's Mill reached and passed its zenith. Everywhere across a two-mile front, victorious Confederate infantry swept through the debris of the battlefield. Fitz John Porter's V Corps, aided by one division from the VI Corps, had failed to hold its position on the high ground north of the Chicka-hominy River. Porter's force had been battling an unfriendly clock as well. It was less than a week removed from the longest day of the year, and the sun did not officially set that day until 7:17 P.M. As long as light lingered, the Southern infantry pressed onward.

Gen. Francis T. Meagher's four regiments, known far and wide as the Irish Brigade, strode into this scene. Always self-confident and aggressive, Meagher's men were the ideal choice for this sort of duty. Capt. George A. Custer, a young staff officer from army headquarters, led the fresh troops across the Chickahominy. Once across, they found the low ground north of the river choked with "fragments of broken regiments," "the remnants of brigades and divisions," and "innumerable wounded."

William J. Nagle of the brigade recalled "flinging away every incumbrance, and with one wild yell" wading through the mass of fugitives. The Irish Brigade had an advantage when it came to stiffening skittish troops. A fleeing Pennsyl-vanian watched and listened as General Meagher deployed that special tool. "I heard him say, 'Steady now, boys; display the green flag.'" When the regiments uncased their trademark banners and struck a belligerent pose, they instantly became a

J. E. B. Stuart.

recognizable and comforting island amidst the thousands of disordered Federals making for the safety of nearby bridges.

While Meagher's men forced their way toward the sound of the guns, the 9th Massachusetts Infantry conducted a fighting withdrawal southward beneath its own green banner. The 9th hailed primarily from around Boston and carried a substantial Irish contingent in its ranks. On June 27, it fought with Charles Griffin's brigade and drew notice for its steadiness on the front line of Porter's position. Lt. Col. Patrick R. Guiney extracted the regiment from its dangerous position in the path of the triumphant Confederates. Although the 9th left the battlefield in good order, it had been badly battered during the day, incurring nearly 250 casualties, including 10 colorbearers, by sunset.

16th New York Volunteer Infantry.

TIM OSTERHELD

RONALD AND JULIE MARRA

53rd New York Volunteers,
D'Epineuil Zouaves.

JO-VAL AND ELDRED CODLING

62nd New York Volunteers,
Anderson Zouaves.

In an unusual episode, the army's famous Irish Brigade unexpectedly met the hard-fighting Massachusetts regiment. The prominent green flags temporarily came together. A member of the 9th harbored fond memories of encounter years later: "They greeted us with rousing cheers which we as heartily returned." Each regiment went its separate way in the gathering darkness. Meagher's entire brigade suffered only a handful of casualties on June 27, and most of the men did not even have an opportunity to discharge their weapons. Nonetheless, Meagher's dramatic arrival at Gaines's Mill helped temper the Union defeat. It did even more to increase the profile of the brigade and to build a reputation destined to be tested at Sharpsburg and Fredericksburg before the year was out.

ROBERT K. KRICK

ARTIST COMMENTS

This painting captured an exceptional moment when two different Irish units, with their exquisite green flags, were concentrated in one location on a battlefield. A rarely perused account of General Meagher's clothing during the Seven Days' Battles provided yet another colorful prospect. Dressed in a suit of dark green velvet trimmed with gold lace and a broad-brimmed straw hat surmounted with a heavy plume, he looked a fitting leader for those brave men.

Through the efforts of a good friend, flag expert Steven Hill, I obtained pictures of the original flag of the 9th, still held by the state of Massachusetts. Painting the lettered presentation inscription in oil paint on this flag took nearly two days of close solid work.

Jackson Is with You

By late afternoon on August 9, 1862, Confederate soldiers under Gen. Thomas J. "Stonewall" Jackson had put in an exhausting day, marching steadily northward into Culpeper County under a pitiless sun. An official weather station a few miles away recorded a temperature of 84 degrees at 7 A.M. and 98 degrees at 2 P.M. According to a Georgian gasping in the heat, it was "the hottest weather I ever experienced; we left men all along the road give out . . . some of them being sun stroke on the road."

When battle erupted that evening along the Culpeper-Orange Pike, road-weary Southern infantry found themselves outflanked and overwhelmed by a surprise attack delivered by determined troops from Connecticut, Pennsylvania, New York, and Wisconsin. Although Jackson enjoyed numerical superiority on the field and had reinforcements drawing near, the Federal onslaught landed at just the right spot to unhinge the Confederate line around the Crittenden Gate.

An Alabamian fighting near the gate wrote home four days later, descriptively if poorly spelled, that "the bawls . . . sung rownd our head like hornits." A New York soldier in the midst of the same maelstrom said that "bullets were thicker than hail stones in a Nebraska cyclone."

Stonewall Jackson dashed into the woods adjacent to the gate in a desperate attempt to rally his unraveling line. Someone handed him a battle flag. With his other hand, the general tried to draw his sword. Finding it rusted into the scabbard, he unclipped the whole thing, scabbard and all, and somehow managed to stay mounted while waving both flag and hardware. Taking advantage of his towering fame, Jackson shouted his own name to catch the attention of wavering men: "Jackson is with you." "Rally, brave men, and press forward." "Jackson will lead you. Follow me!"

In response to Jackson's exhortations, Confederates forgot their weariness and drove forward, "sweeping the fields and mowing down the Yankees before us," a participant gloated, "as if they were only blackbirds before the sportsman." A captain in the renowned Stonewall Brigade wrote in a contemporary letter that when Jackson "waved his hand . . . the men became wild with excitement, and with cheers that must have made Genl Pope tremble, swept forward. . . . It was a perfect Jubilee, rather than a battle at that moment."

DAVID R. RANKIN JR.

The Watson Flying Battery, New Orleans.

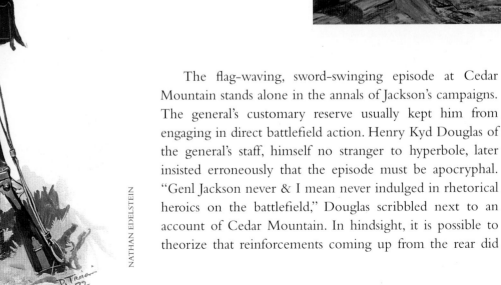

NATHAN EDELSTEIN

*13th Pennsylvania Reserves
(The Bucktails).*

The flag-waving, sword-swinging episode at Cedar Mountain stands alone in the annals of Jackson's campaigns. The general's customary reserve usually kept him from engaging in direct battlefield action. Henry Kyd Douglas of the general's staff, himself no stranger to hyperbole, later insisted erroneously that the episode must be apocryphal. "Genl Jackson never & I mean never indulged in rhetorical heroics on the battlefield," Douglas scribbled next to an account of Cedar Mountain. In hindsight, it is possible to theorize that reinforcements coming up from the rear did

Steady on the Colors.

more to turn the battle than the men Jackson rallied in the thickets near the gate. Nonetheless, Stonewall's personal, visceral involvement in the dramatic moment prompted him to tell his wife that he judged Cedar Mountain to be "the most successful of his exploits."

ROBERT K. KRICK

ARTIST COMMENTS

Although they don't really appear to advantage, I used more individual models for this painting than any other. As always,

photos were taken on the authentic location, and the details were carefully double-checked with famed historian Robert K. Krick, who suggested this topic. The model for Stonewall was posed with an original Model 1850 staff officer's sword in its metal scabbard, which he found nearly impossible to keep raised for more than a few moments at a time. The genuine incident certainly could not have lasted more than a fleeting instant, owing to the weight of the sheathed weapon. Jackson's flag is one of the earlier silk patterns, which were in fact a pink hue, not the typical red.

DIEHARDS

For the fledgling Manassas Gap Railroad, the proposed rail line stretching from Gainesville to Alexandria, Virginia, offered the railroad its best chance to compete on equal footing with its primary rival, the Orange and Alexandria. But by 1858, one year from completion and with rails for the new line stockpiled in Alexandria, work had ceased. The railroad line would remain unfinished and almost forgotten until August 1862, mainly because of the financial uncertainties of the coming Civil War.

In what became known as the second battle of Bull Run or Second Manassas, the veteran troops of Confederate major general Thomas Jackson's corps found themselves fighting fiercely to hold on to the cuts and fills of the unfinished line. Just as determined to dislodge Jackson's men were 10,000 battle-hardened veterans of three Union divisions, under the overall command of Maj. Gen. Fitz John Porter.

Massed in the Groveton woods, east of the Groveton Sudley Road, the Union troops waited anxiously for the advance to begin, enjoying what little cover the woods could provide from the incessant Confederate artillery fire. To their front across an open field lay the unfinished railroad and less-than-hospitable inhabitants. "The embankment of broken stone and gravel," recalled one Union soldier, "had been reconstructed in a most formidable work of defense. Along the top of that railroad embankment there was a gleam of musket barrels, as they were aimed towards us and resting on it."

On the Union right, only 300 yards separated the combatants, this distance increased to more than a half mile on the Union left. Covering this open ground were the eighteen Confederate cannons of Col. S. D. Lee's artillery battalion. Well positioned on the Brawner farm, Lee's artillerymen were prepared to offer a warm welcome to any soul who ventured into the open. By 3 P.M., all the preparations had been made, and with three deafening cheers, Porter's men poured out of the woods. All along the

Picture, jacket, and bullet with bone fragment removed from the leg of Edward N. Fulton of Baxter's Zouaves following the battle of Antietam.
TROIANI COLLECTION

Confederate line, cries of "Here they come!" were heard. Recalling the event years later, one Virginian wrote, "Every man in our line shifted his cartridge box to the front, unstrapped it and his cap box, gave his gun a second look, and took his position to meet the enemy."

On leaving the woods, the Federal troops were met with a perfect tempest of shot and shell. "Now the bullets began to fly about our ears, recalled one New Yorker, "and men to pitch forwards or backwards out of the line to the earth." Onward the blue lines rushed, all the while receiving severe enfilading artillery fire from S. D. Lee's hard-worked cannons. The New Yorkers of Sullivan's brigade succeeded in running this gauntlet, only to find their momentum stymied at the

railroad embankment by the intense fire of Brig. Gen. W. E. Starke's Louisianans. The "yells from both sides were indescribably savage," recalled one New Yorker.

For the Louisianans, the Union onslaught was bringing them close to collapse. The constant pressure of the Federal advance resulted in the rapid depletion of ammunition. The few rounds that the men could scrounge up from the dead and wounded were quickly fired, and with bayonets fixed, the boys of the Pelican State waited for the inevitable Union rush over the embankment. Not yet ready to concede the contest, Lieutenant O'Keefe, an Irishman in the 1st Louisiana yelled, "Boys, give them the rocks." Needing no further encouragement, the embattled Confederates grabbed stones

DR. DAVID YANKE

New York Independent Battalion, Les Enfants Perdus.

and starting hurling them at their counterparts on the reverse slope. For those few stalwart Union soldiers still clinging to the embankment, this introduction of a new, though primitive, weapon broke what will they had to continue the fight. Those that could made their way back to Union lines; the remainder soon found themselves in the hands of the Confederate victors.

For the Confederates, General Porter's attack had come dangerously close to succeeding. For the Union forces, the repulse of Porter's attack was just the beginning of a series of events that ultimately led to one of the most decisive Confederate victories of the American Civil War.

KEITH KNOKE

ARTIST COMMENTS

A posed throw is never as good as the real thing. Therefore, my superb models spent a solid afternoon doing real-time and slow-motion rock throwing while in full uniform. I was told there were sore arms a-plenty the next day. For the stretcher team, a real group with a stretcher was set up to re-create this episode, with the bearers loading, lifting, and carrying for a good while.

SONS OF ERIN

The 69th New York was raised in the fall of 1861 as the senior regiment in Gen. Thomas Meagher's famed Irish Brigade, its men drawn from the teeming immigrant Irish Catholic population of New York City.

On the morning of September 17, 1862, the 69th, already worn down to a mere 330 men after savage fighting on the Peninsula that summer, found themselves camped on the eastern bank of Antietam Creek just outside Sharpsburg, Maryland. Shortly after breakfast, Maj. Gen. "Fighting Dick" Richardson, their division commander, gave the order to move. With the 69th leading the brigade and the division, they crossed the Antietam at Pry's Ford. Some men removed their shoes and socks for the crossing, though others were already barefoot from the hard marching they had done in the summer of 1862.

Heading southwest, the Irish arrived at the edge of a cornfield, where they threw off everything but their muskets and cartridge boxes. Already, distant Confederate artillery and sharpshooters on their flanks were making themselves felt, though this was little compared with what the Irish suffered when they paused to tear down the fence that divided the cornfield from a field of clover that lay beyond. The men lay down to escape the fire as the slow and deadly work of dismantling the fence was accomplished by skirmishers, but immediately thereafter, they were up in their lines again and ready to advance.

The flags snapped sharply in the breeze that warm day, creating distinct patterns of light and shadow in the folds of the embroidered silk banners. Gen. Francis T. Meagher and two of his staff officers led the way toward the sunken country road where Maj. Gen. D. H. Hill's Confederate division awaited them. Mounted on his magnificent bright bay, Meagher was decked out in a splendid uniform with a gold shoulder belt. With raised sword, he ordered the disciplined battle lines forward on the double quick, but not before the faithful brigade chaplain, Father Corby, took the opportunity to

The late 69th New York Regimental historian Ken Powers visiting Don's studio.

bestow absolution on the men. He rode quickly across the front of the moving ranks with raised arm, asking the men to make an act of contrition. They removed their caps and bowed their heads as the priest passed. The rosary fingered by the soldier at the extreme right of the picture gives testimony to the faith that sustained these Irish soldiers.

Their lines then surged forward with wild Irish cheers, until they were within just thirty yards of the intense Confederate fire coming from the sunken road that would ever after be known as Bloody Lane. Pouring volley upon volley of buck and ball ammunition from their smoothbore muskets in the lane, the 69th held its honored but dangerously exposed position on the extreme right of the division until the few men left standing were finally relieved by Caldwell's brigade. By that time, General Meagher had been carried senseless from the field after his horse was shot from under him. The 69th fared much worse. Nearly 60 percent of the regiment fell that day, including its brave commander, Lt. Col. James Kelly. Eight men went down while bearing the green flag, and the last, his clothes and flag riddled by bullets, had but half a staff to grasp, as the intense fire had cut it in two.

The 69th's reputation for dependability and valor always seemed to put them where the action was hottest. These gallant Sons of Erin paid dearly for that reputation on America's bloodiest day.

LAWRENCE F. KOHL

ARTIST COMMENTS

Creating a long battle line that looks convincing requires a good bit of ingenuity. Having a finite number of models, I concentrated first on the figures in front that are most visible to viewers. Each model was used once here. Since the men in the rear ranks are partly blocked by those in front, I was able to redress the same models and use them again for the next row. It was important to redress them completely to help create the illusion that they are different men. I had to change the other kinds of muskets in the painting process. Using about eighteen to twenty models, I was able to build an entire regiment and never use the same face twice. Although I could easily alter faces to look different, to me it never looks as convincing as a portrait of a real person. I had only two Model 1842 muskets and three New York State jackets, which I kept on the models in front. The crucifix held by the soldier on the right was loaned to my by my old friend Bruce Hermann, whose great-grandfather had carried it.

Reference field trip photos of the Sunken Road.

UNTIL SUNDOWN

Since first light, it had been peaceful for Col. John B. Gordon and his 6th Alabama. For some four hours that Wednesday morning of September 17, 1862, they had watched the fighting develop a mile or so to the north of them and listened to the rising thunder of musketry and artillery there, wondering when their turn might come. They had taken their present posting on this little farm road between Sharpsburg and Antietam Creek two days earlier. The day before that, September 14, they had been in a stiff fight at Turner's Gap in nearby South Mountain.

Gordon's 6th Alabama was part of Brig. Gen. Robert Rodes's brigade, which was part of Maj. Gen. D. H. Hill's division, which was part of Gen. Robert E. Lee's Army of Northern Virginia, and the Alabamians knew each officer in that chain of command to be the hardest kind of fighter.

It was an article of faith in the 6th Alabama that Colonel Gordon had a charmed life. He personally led the regiment in every battle and was never hit. "They can't hurt him," the men said. "He's as safe one place as another." At Seven Pines outside Richmond in May, 59 percent of the men were killed or wounded, and Gordon was the only field officer in the regiment still alive when the battle was over. (Not surprisingly, the 6th Alabama went into battle at Sharpsburg with the "Seven Pines" stitched on its flag.) A month later,

1st Company Richmond Howitzers.

leading a charge at Malvern Hill, Gordon counted seven bullet holes in his uniform and not a scratch otherwise. After that, he wrote, "a sort of blind faith possessed my men that I was not to be killed in battle."

This position at the center of General Lee's long battle line was a good one to defend. Over the years, heavy travel and erosion had worn down the surface of the farm road until it resembled a shallow trench, and the men strengthened it further by turning the split-rail fence on the side facing the enemy into a rough breastwork. To reach the road,

the Yankees would have to cross a low rise in front, silhouetting themselves against the skyline. On the military maps, the position was called simply the Sunken Road. It would soon earn a grim fame by another name—Bloody Lane.

A few minutes before 9 A.M., General Lee himself suddenly appeared at the 6th Alabama's position. The regiment was at the center of the Sunken Road line, making it the center of the whole army. The rest of Rodes's brigade was in the road to the left, and Brig. Gen. George B. Anderson's brigade of North Carolinians was to the right. Lee's center was naturally strong but thinly manned—only these two brigades and a scattering of other men of D. H. Hill's division, altogether just 2,500 infantry—and the commanding general felt the need to brace the defenders to their task. He had already seen the Yankees forming up in strength and moving their way.

Lee had injured his hands and wrists in a fall some days before, the right seriously enough to require a sling, and managing his horse, Traveller, was difficult, but nonetheless, he greatly impressed the men as an imposing martial figure. Riding with him on his tour of the line was dark-bearded D. H. Hill, the division commander, and mustachioed Robert Rodes, the brigade commander. Lee warned Gordon that the enemy's attack would surely be a determined one; he must hold the Sunken Road at any sacrifice.

Hardly fifteen minutes later, the Yankees came, waves of them. First was William H. French's division of the II Corps. The Confederates responded with a murderous volley. "The effect was appalling," Gordon remembered. "The entire front line, with few exceptions, went down in the consuming blast." The Rebel fire, said another man, "brought down the enemy as grain falls before a reaper." Each of French's three brigades attacked in turn and each was wrecked. Then came the brigades of Maj. Gen. Israel B. Richardson's II Corps division. Rodes's and Anderson's men stood up to every assault.

Yet the defenders were taking costly losses as well. John Gordon's charmed life was gravely threatened, as two bullets struck him in the right leg, another in the left arm, and another in the shoulder. He somehow remained standing, encouraging his men on the firing line. He reminded them of his promise to hold until sunset. But the sun, he later wrote, "moved very slowly; in fact, it seemed to stand still." Then a fifth bullet struck him, this one in the face. He collapsed, with his bleeding face in his cap; only another Yankee bullet that had ripped open his cap prevented him from suffocating in his own blood.

Gordon was carried from the field, and a subsequent mix-up in orders caused the 6th Alabama to give up the Sunken Road. Yet farther back, with a last desperate, convulsive effort, the Rebels managed to hold Lee's center intact. There would be no breakthrough here. At last, darkness ended the bloodiest single day's fighting in the nation's history. Colonel Gordon's pledge to hold "till the sun goes down" was made good.

STEPHEN W. SEARS

ARTIST COMMENTS

Areas of the Bloody Lane still present an appearance very similar to that of 1862, which was an extraordinary advantage in re-creating this scene accurately. The great character model with a beard reminded me of a country preacher, so he was posed reading to his flock from an original soldier's pocket Bible from my collection. I consulted closely with historians Dr. Joe Harsh and John Hennessy on Lee's appearance and the condition of his arm in a sling.

Models pose as wounded Union soldiers.

BATTERY LONGSTREET

As the Confederate line east of Sharpsburg unraveled on September 17, 1862, several senior officers placed themselves in conspicuous positions to help strengthen the defense. The army commander, Gen. Robert E. Lee, personally rallied troops, and the cavalry commander, Maj. Gen. Jeb Stuart, closely supervised artillery. Gen. James Longstreet, one of Lee's top subordinates, found himself in an even more urgent situation that called for leadership of a different stripe.

The Federal II Corps had flanked the Confederates out of the Bloody Lane and pressed onward through the fields toward the Piper fields and farmhouse. Remnants of ten Southern brigades blocked the way, often fighting in disjointed clumps. Longstreet and his staff caromed through the middle of this, encouraging men at several locations. Near the Piper orchard, the general's party found two cannons from the 3rd Company of the Washington Artillery, a famous command led by Capt. Merritt B. "Buck" Miller. The incoming enemy fire was accurate, wrote an infantryman serving with the battery, and the men of the gun crews "were dropping down it seemed every two or three minutes." The steady casualties and heavy fire had driven off many of the cannoneers, leaving the guns silent. General Longstreet watched approvingly as his entourage, which included some of the most important staff officers in the Army of Northern Virginia, dismounted and got the cannons into action once again.

Perhaps no more distinguished gun crew ever assembled on a Civil War battlefield. Its members included Maj. G. Moxley Sorrel, soon to be the chief of staff for the Confederate I Corps; Maj. Thomas J. Walton, Longstreet's commissary officer; Lt. Col. Peyton T. Manning, in charge of Longstreet's ordnance; Maj. John W. Fairfax; and Lt. Thomas J. Goree. Beside them, spotting the effect of the fire, sat Longstreet. A correspondent from the army described the general in the autumn of 1862 as "stout and fleshy, and of good height," wearing "a quiet, courageous look." Now he showed animation, "talked earnestly and gesticulated" while his aides and a few of the original Washington Artillery men worked the guns. A Georgia infantryman happened upon the unusual sight and paused long enough to notice that Longstreet "was sure putting the shells where they would do the most good." "Our fire was really strong and effective," wrote a proud Major Sorrel. The ersatz artillerists soon gave way to the real gunners, who had reorganized sufficiently to return to duty. "We mounted again with cheerful grins at our sudden adventure," Sorrel said. Longstreet and his young staff officers had cause for satisfaction. They had not saved the day by themselves, certainly, yet their spontaneous work had bolstered one portion of a sagging Confederate line.

Episodes of this sort occurred with some frequency in the critical minutes at Sharpsburg. They aided in blunting the Union advances in several places, but they also contributed to the blossoming spirit of Lee's army, and in time some of the day's heroics became cherished tales among the army's veterans.

ROBERT E. L. KRICK

ARTIST COMMENTS

Trees have always been difficult for me, particularly pines. A photography trip to a local orchard helped with the setting here, but the trees of the Civil War era were not as large or healthy as the robust examples of today. Therefore, I had to paint them somewhat smaller and more scraggly to truly depict a typical fruit orchard of the mid-nineteenth century. The orchard that stood in for this project was a bit neglected, which helped.

Lone Star

The morning of September 17, 1862, found the 226 officers and men of Lt. Col. Phillip A. Work's 1st Texas Infantry in a foul mood. As part of the famed Hood's Texas Brigade, the regiment was footsore and no doubt fatigued from its recent participation in the Confederate efforts to hold the South Mountain passes and oppose the initial Union crossing of Antietam Creek. Despite the incessant Union artillery raining down on their position just north of Sharpsburg, Maryland, the Texans were determined to get their first hot meal in days. The early-morning arrival of Union major general Joseph Hooker's I Corp opposite the Confederate left,

however, brought a less-than-satisfying end to the well-deserved meal.

Consisting of the 18th Georgia, Hampton's Legion, and the 1st, 4th, and 5th Texas Infantry, Hood's Texas Brigade, now under the command of Col. William T. Wofford, was ordered to fall in and be prepared to support the already hard-pressed troops of Maj. Gen. Thomas J. Jackson's Corps. They would not have long to wait. At 7 A.M., the Confederate divisional commander, Brig. Gen. John B. Hood, received an urgent call for support and immediately put Col. Evander M. Law's brigade and Hood's Texas Brigade in motion.

Marching in line of battle and passing the small white Dunker church, the 1st Texas advanced with its cherished Lone Star flag leading the way.

Crossing the Hagerstown Pike, Hood's division entered the pasture located south of David R. Miller's cornfield. Recalling the arrival of Hood's division, one Union colonel wrote, "A long and steady line of rebel gray, unbroken by the fugitives who fly before us, comes sweeping down through woods around the church. They raise the yell and fire. It was like a scythe running through our line." Hood's division slammed into the unorganized Union forces in the pasture, driving them back into the East Woods and Miller cornfield. True to form, the aggressive Hood pressed his advantage, directing Colonel Law's brigade with the 5th Texas in tow to clear the East Woods and eastern portion of the Miller cornfield; the 4th Texas to secure the division's left flank along the Hagerstown Pike; and the remaining regiments of Hood's Texas Brigade to follow up on the Union retreat and clear the Miller cornfield.

Raising the Rebel yell, the Hampton Legion, 18th Georgia, and 1st Texas crashed into the cornfield in mad pursuit of the Union forces. Quickly outpacing the other two regiments, and with Lieutenant Colonel Work unable to check its advance, the 1st Texas rushed for the northern terminus of the cornfield. On they rushed, "One two, even three may fall in touch," recalled one Texan, "but on [we] go conscious of but one thing and that is to conquer or die."

Reaching the northern edge of the cornfield, the charge of the 1st Texas was met with a devastating volley let loose from a brigade of waiting Pennsylvanians. Staggered but undaunted, the Texans returned fire. The contest now became one of attrition, with each side trading blow for blow. However, determined the Texans were to hold their hard-won ground, the massive number of casualties the regiment was receiving and the real possibility of their left flank being turned left Work with but one alternative, and that was to retreat. Slowly and deliberately, the Texans backed themselves out of the cornfield and returned to the Dunker church.

In the days and weeks following the battle, the magnitude of the regiment's sacrifice in the Miller cornfield became shockingly apparent. Of the 226 men who followed the Lone Star banner into battle, 186 were counted among the casualties—over 82 percent. The 1st Texas thus earned the distinction of suffering the most casualties proportional to the number engaged of any regiment, North or South.

KEITH KNOKE

ARTIST COMMENTS
Since corn was a major visual factor in this scene, only a real cornfield would do for rendering it. I recalled the legendary story about the famed French painter Meissionier, who actually galloped horsemen through tall rye to see exactly how the trampled grass would appear. I made a deal with a local farmer: In exchange for a print, he would let me demolish a small corner of his cornfield with my models. There was absolutely no substitute for seeing the real thing and how the models looked while standing or lying among the crushed stalks. I took some of the ears and stalks back to my studio to have by the easel for detail work. I'm always carting branches, rocks, and other outdoor organic material into the studio, to my wife's horror.

Reference field trip photo of Burnside's Bridge.

BURNSIDE'S BRIDGE

By the late morning of September 17, 1862, Union major general George B. McClellan was not at all pleased with the progress of the Union IX Corps' attempt to press the Confederate right flank at the battle of Antietam. Standing between the IX Corp and its objective was Antietam Creek and 300 battle-hardened veterans of the 2nd and 20th Georgia Volunteer Infantry Regiments. Although vastly outnumbered, the Georgians took advantage of the high ground along the west bank of the Antietam and thus were well positioned to defend the Rohrbach Bridge, the most likely Union crossing point. The strong defensive nature of the Confederates' position was not lost on their Union antagonist. "No point of attack on the whole field," recalled Union brigadier general Jacob D. Cox, "was unpromising as this."

Not one to be deterred by a strong Confederate position, as he would clearly show three months later at the battle of Fredericksburg, Maj. Gen. Ambrose Burnside ordered the Rohrbach Bridge taken and the Confederates on the west bank cleared. The events of the next five hours proved that would be no easy task. Measuring 125 feet long and a mere 12 feet wide, the Rohrbach Bridge, soon to bear the name of the general ordering its capture, became a bottleneck to the Union advance. The first in a series of ill-planned and ill-fated attempts to take the bridge was ventured by the 11th Connecticut Volunteer Infantry. Rushing for the bridge and withstanding a devastating storm of bullets, the 11th was successful in reaching the bridge, only to learn that its promised supports were not coming, and it was forced to retire. Next in line was the brigade of Brig. Gen. James Nagle. Two of his regiments, the 2nd Maryland and 6th New Hampshire, made a daring charge toward the

Wooden battlefield tombstone of soldier of the 2nd Georgia killed while defending Burnside's Bridge at Antietam.

bridge, only to be stopped short by the intense fire of the Georgians. A second charge by the same two regiments only a short time later had no better results.

Col. Edward Ferrero's brigade, consisting of the 21st and 35th Massachusetts, 51st New York, and 51st Pennsylvania Regiments, was next in line to break the stalemate at the bridge. Determined to succeed and not repeat the mistakes of his predecessors, Ferrero promised the 51st New York and 51st Pennsylvania as much whiskey as they wanted if they were successful in taking the bridge. Needing little further encouragement, the two regiments soon made a dash for the bridge. Although they intended to rush across the span, the severe Confederate fire forced the regiments to take cover, with the 51st Pennsylvania going to the north and 51st New York going to the south of the bridge.

It was the moment of truth. The regiments had lost the momentum of the charge and were now pinned down on either side of the bridge. They could move forward or fall back, but staying where they were was not feasible. They chose the former, removing the fence rails nearest the mouth of the bridge. Both regiments poured onto the bridge, rushing to the other side and driving the Georgians before them. The two 51st regiments were successful in taking the bridge, and true to his word, Ferrero rewarded the regiments with whiskey.

KEITH KNOKE

ARTIST COMMENTS

For me, the challenge of a panoramic scene is to avoid the look of an ant colony, without a central focus. Here, it was important to show most of the bridge in order to give the viewer a sense of exactly what was unfolding. But the more of the bridge that was included, the smaller the figures would become. The answer was to crop the left approach to the bridge and concentrate on just the attack of the 51st Pennsylvania. It is tempting to try to cram everything that happened onto the canvas, but the artist may sacrifice the drama of the event to do so.

Emblems of Valor.

"GARRYOWEN"

Since the time of Julius Caesar's famous decision to cross the Rubicon in 49 A.D., moving armies across rivers has posed tactical and logistical difficulties to commanders. American troops had crossed many a river to get at an enemy in the years before 1862—most famously, Washington's celebrated crossing of the Delaware. Until the battle of Fredericksburg, however, no major American army had fought its way across a river to establish a bridgehead in preparation for crossing the main force by a temporary bridge.

On December 11, 1862, Northern troops, prevented by a hail of musketry from completing pontoon bridges across the 420-foot-wide Rappahannock River, resorted to rowing the pontoon boats to the far bank and driving away their tormentors. That brave and daring initiative made possible completion of the bridges.

By the next morning, fighting in town had ended. Only a smattering of indirect, long-range fire dropped into the vicinity of the crossing point. At about 10:30 A.M., the Irish Brigade moved briskly in column, four abreast, onto the bridge at a double quick and headed for Fredericksburg. A beaming sun brightened the cool morning, promising warmth to break the icy grip of the preceding week. Ice still

Stack of original Civil War drums in the studio.

clung to the river's edge, built up by unseasonable cold, which now gave way to Indian summer.

As the Irish Brigade reached the right bank of the Rappahannock, a small Zouave band struck up the lilting strains of "Garryowen." That rollicking drinking tune apparently had been adopted by the Royal Irish Lancers when stationed in the Limerick suburb of Garryowen in the eighteenth century. The lancers later carried the song with them to Portugal, where they served under Wellington. In 1862, the music remained relatively unfamiliar in North America. Soon after the Civil War, the 7th U.S. Cavalry adopted "Garryowen" as its regimental music, playing it steadily through a series of famous campaigns of differing success. Mrs. George A. Custer said she believed that Capt. Myles W. Keogh, an 1862 immigrant to North America, introduced "Garryowen" to her husband, who thereafter often hummed and whistled the tune.

The knot of officers at the city end of the bridges, watching the Irishmen cross, included their brigadier, Thomas F. Meagher, and division commander, Gen. Winfield Scott Hancock. Most of the brigade adored Meagher as a resplendent Irish hero, though many of them probably had deduced by this time that he was nothing remotely like a reincarnation of Bonaparte. They recognized in Hancock a superb combat commander, well on his way to becoming perhaps the best fighting general in the Army of the Potomac. The brigade's bands sometimes played "Hail to the Chief" when Hancock came into view.

After crossing the river in a nominally westward direction, the Irish Brigade veered south on the street paralleling the river and moved well down toward the lower end of town. To the men's disgust, "professional embalmers" who followed the army, "alive to business, thrust their cards into the hands of the men as they went along." The vulpine businessmen might have been an omen of what lay ahead for the Irishmen on December 13, as they marched toward what a brigade chaplain called "simply a slaughter-pen."

Early on the twelfth, as the Irish Brigade paraded on the Federal side of the river, preparing to cross, an Irish officer marveled at the martial splendor of the army around him. Capt. John H. Donovan of the 69th New York described later how, with prideful awe, he admired "the bright banners and innumerable battalions" and knew that "certain victory awaited this army." "I was not aware," he mused, "that hell personified was so close at hand and ready for our destruction." Donovan, who already had lost an eye at Malvern Hill, went down badly wounded on December 13, one of 545 men in the Irish Brigade killed, wounded, or missing. The men who had whistled "Garryowen" cheerfully on December 12 faced a dreadful ordeal—"hell personified"—the next day.

ROBERT K. KRICK

Irish Brigade recruiting poster.

ARTIST COMMENTS

Using a midriver viewpoint made arranging the composition for this painting difficult. This was solved by good friends Edward McGee and Fredericksburg gallery owner Joe Fulginiti, who floated out into the Rappahanock River in a rubber raft on the anniversary of the crossing, at the same time of day, to shoot the pictures for me. Another problem was re-creating the stone Scott house, which was torn down shortly after the battle, having been heavily damaged by artillery fire. Fortunately, a period sketch and a photograph showing the remaining foundation still existed, which formed the basis for my artistic reconstruction. For the details of the bridge, I consulted *Duane's Manual for Engineer Troops* and wartime photographs of bridges. Close study of the original images showed that in nearly every case, dirt was spread on the planks, probably to establish a nonskid layer on a potentially wet surface. Unlike recent movie depictions, the regiments crossed the bridge at a run to avoid Confederate artillery fire at the Falmouth bridgehead approach.

BRONZE GUNS AND IRON MEN

The geological forces that created the Rappahannock River valley near Fredricksburg left behind a virtual amphitheater. High ground hugs the river on its left bank and looks across a mile or so of flat tidal river plain at similar heights behind the town of Fredericksburg. In December 1862, a Northern host was in the town and on the plain, and Gen. Robert E. Lee's Confederate Army of Northern Virginia looked down on them confidently from a connected line of ridges seven miles long.

The young artillerist John Pelham was born in Calhoun County, Alabama, and got his education at the U.S. Military Academy at West Point. He matriculated at West Point in 1856, in one of the few classes that faced a five-year curriculum before that experimental system was abandoned. Because of the five-year schedule, and because Alabama seceded so early in 1861, Pelham never graduated from the academy. His commission as lieutenant of artillery in Confederate services was dated March 16, 1861, just a couple months before his quondam comrades at West Point were to graduate.

Pelham was assigned to duty with Alburtis's battery, Virginia Light Artillery. He commanded that battery at First Manassas and won mention in the official report of Thomas

J. Jackson, newly christened "Stonewall." John Pelham won promotion to captain and permanent command of his own battery on March 23, 1862, just over a year after he had entered Confederate service. A few months later, on August 9, Pelham's stellar service earned him the single collar star of a major.

Pelham surely must have been the most frequently described junior officer in the Confederacy. One of his contemporaries at West Point, who became a Confederate general, described Pelham as "a very young looking, handsome & attractive fellow, slender, blue eyes, light hair, smooth, red & white complexion." This witness went on to report that Pelham's "modest and refined expression" was such that his close acquaintances "never spoke of him but as 'Sallie.'"

Pelham's storied achievements on many fields were a fitting preface to his climactic performance on the morning of Saturday, December 13, 1862. Federals in large numbers had crossed the Rappahannock on pontoon bridges during the previous two days. Confederates awaited them in a strong position behind a railroad embankment, in front of which lay a broad field almost half a mile wide. It was a stark killing ground across which the Federals must advance, but the Northern advantage in numbers and weight of artillery neutralized most of the Southern guns.

As the first major infantry assault by the Northerners got started, Confederates were cheered and Federals were startled by the sudden barking of a defiant gun that enfiladed the attackers' line. It was Pelham, with one Napoleon of the Virginia horse artillery battery commanded by Capt. Mathias Winston Henry.

For a time, two pieces of Pelham's horse artillery fired, but one of them—a Blakely—soon went quiet. The solitary Napoleon kept up its roar despite a torrent of Federal fire hurled in its direction. Pelham took advantage of what cover the ground offered and moved repeatedly in a desperate attempt to avoid destruction. Tens of thousands of Southern onlookers held their breath while annoyed Federal hordes muttered under theirs. One onlooker summarized the affair in a single succinct sentence: "The enemy were in dense masses advancing straight toward our line of Battle & Pelham was exactly on their left flank with his Gun with no support whatever."

Pelham was using solid shot primarily because of the devastating psychological effect such rounds had when crashing in from the side on a long line of troops. Even so, he managed to "blow up a caisson for the Yankees" with a fortunate round.

When Pelham eventually was ordered to retire from his exposed position and the famous episode ended, his fighting on this bloody day had only begun. The youthful major was placed in charge of a mélange of guns drawn from various sources, with the mission of continuing his flanking fire against the Federal lines from a somewhat safer and more oblique angle. Although this later service by Pelham lasted for several hours and was of considerable importance, it has not received the attention that has been given to the desperate drama of the single gun. The later fighting was just as bitter, however, as attested by the testimony of a member of Stuart's staff who said Pelham's position was "the hottest place" he had ever visited. The staff captain found Pelham standing between two busy guns, and "the shells were crashing in every direction."

Accolades poured in on John Pelham. Stuart, Jackson, A. P. Hill, and others praised the youthful major both officially and unofficially. Lee himself penned the best-known praise when he used a happily turned phrase in referring to "the gallant Pelham"—no given name, no rank, just "the gallant." Since Lee's official reports usually were couched in reserved language, this departure must have thrilled the young horse artillerist. Even more than a century later, historians read Lee's quiet and drab reports carefully in search of nuances about subordinates, often in vain. Against that backdrop, "the gallant Pelham" stands brightly limned.

Pelham was destined to die just ninety-four days after his great feat at Fredericksburg. At the height of a thundering charge of Virginia cavalrymen near Kelly's Ford on March 17, 1863, Pelham went down when a piece of shell went through his head, crushing his skull.

ROBERT K. KRICK

ARTIST COMMENTS

This painting convinced me that I needed to have my own artillery park. I had to meet the models in New Jersey at the house of a collector who owned the original Napoleon, and we did the shoot on his lawn. Traveling to photograph the artillery made me dependent on the weather and various other people's timetables, which often delayed shooting sessions. Although some artists may pose the models separately from the gun, I prefer to set up the entire scene with everyone in place. Otherwise, it's impossible to determine details such as how the gunner's shadows might fall across the spokes of the wheel or the size relationships between the crew and piece. As collecting opportunities arose, I bit the financial bullet and purchased several original Civil War cannons, complete with all the equipment. Now I can pose everything right here in the yard, exactly the way I need it.

FIRE ON CAROLINE STREET

The morning December 11, 1862, found the 20th Massachusetts Volunteer Infantry on the east bank of the Rappahannock River, opposite the Confederate-held city of Fredericksburg, Virginia. As the troops approached the river, it became apparent that Maj. Gen. Ambrose Burnside's long-awaited attempt to take the city had begun. Having been selected to lead the Union forces across the northern or uppermost pontoon bridge, the Bay State men were in fine spirits. "The cannonade had already begun," recalled Maj. George Macy, acting commander of the 20th Massachusetts, "and never was there a more beautiful sight. . . . The moon was just setting and the sun rising, while a thick mist enveloped everything."

Working under the cover of this mist was the 50th New York Engineer Regiment, feverishly trying to complete the upper pontoon bridge. With the lifting of the fog and the early-morning light, however, came the inevitable musketry fire of Confederate brigadier general William Barksdale's Mississippians. The progress of bridge building at the upper crossing came to a sudden halt. Throughout the morning and afternoon, the Mississippians succeeded in slowing, if not stopping, work on the bridge.

With daylight fading and few apparent alternatives, Union commanders opted to send infantry across the river in the yet-to-be used pontoons scows. Following behind, the 7th Michigan and 19th and 20th Massachusetts boarded the pontoon scows, no doubt recalling a similar river crossing they made fourteen months earlier at the battle of Ball's Bluff. Little did they know that many of the soldiers that had driven them into the Potomac River at that disastrous battle were desperately trying to do the same here at Fredericksburg.

Once across the river, the 20th Massachusetts was placed in defensive position along the west bank of the Rappahannock, only to be ordered forward a short while later. Needing to expand the bridgehead, Major Macy was ordered to "clear the street leading from the bridge at all hazards." Forming into column by company, the regiment left the river and marched west up Hawke Street. Macy halted the column for a brief moment and tried in vain to encourage the 7th Michigan to join in the advance. Unsuccessful, the enraged Macy decided to press on alone. Concealed behind fences or houses, or looking through doors or windows, Barksdale's Mississippians watched the Massachusetts regiment advance. "They moved forward in splendid style," recalled a soldier in the 13th Mississippi. "It was a magnificent sight, which won the admiration of the Mississippians." With Capt. Henry Abbott's Company I leading the way, the 20th Massachusetts had barely gotten under way when the Mississippians unleashed a volley that staggered the column. "Our men began dropping at every point," said a soldier in Company I. "Where men fell and left a vacant place other men stepped into their places. . . . There was not a man who faltered."

Captain Abbott pushed his men through the intersection of Hawke and Caroline Streets, ordering them to return fire only when a target presented itself. Companies K and A, being next in column, entered the intersection and wheeled south and north, respectively. "Here we cleared the houses near us," wrote Major Macy, "but shot came from far and near, we could see no one and were simply murdered." The massed formation of the 20th Massachusetts provided an inviting target to the Mississippians, who by one count inflicted ninety-seven casualties in and around the intersection. Despite the staggering number of casualties and the stubborn resistance of the Mississippians, the 20th managed to hold their ground. With arrival of other Federal forces and the onset of darkness, the Mississippians faded back into the night, bringing to an end the fiercest urban fighting to occur during the American Civil War.

KEITH KNOKE

ARTIST COMMENTS

Street scenes are always the worst to re-create, particularly when buildings no longer exist and must be depicted from verbal descriptions. The brick building at the right side of the picture was mentioned in period Fredericksburg insurance reports but is no longer extant. In order to fill the gap, Joe Fulginiti found a surviving house similar to the one described in the report to

use as a stand-in. This ensured that the house in the painting would have the correct type of regional architecture and structural detail.

I had suspected that the 20th Massachusetts had gray overcoats at this time but couldn't substantiate it. The 19th had them, as did the 21st, and the 20th was equipped at the same time. being equipped at the same time. I finally found it written in the regimental history of the 21st that at Freder–icksburg, "the 20th Massachusetts, owing to their gray over-

coats, had been fired into as rebels on the afternoon of the crossing." Contrary to popular belief, not all Federal regi-ments were issued sky blue overcoats at this period of the war. Because of material shortages, contractors had been allowed to supply, gray, dark blue, black, and possibly other colors. As less fighting was done in winter, colors of overcoats were not as critical. By the winter of 1863–64, the remainder of these disliked and potentially hazardous garments were long out of service.

Joshua L. Chamberlain

ARTIST COMMENTS

Having grown weary of consistently erroneous artistic and film portrayals of Joshua L. Chamberlain, especially with concise information readily available, I decided that an accurate portrait needed to be made. Despite a movie depiction to the contrary, the 20th Maine was not heavily engaged in the battle and spent much of the time hunkered down on the field, and there is no record of Chamberlain firing a shot at the Confederates, who were ridiculously out of range of his pistol.

Chamberlain's own writings to his wife describe his appearance at the time of Fredericksburg:

> *Picture yourself a stout looking fellow—face covered with a beard—with a pair of cavalry pants on—sky blue—big enough for Goliath, and as coarse as a sheep's back—said fellow having worn storm and ridden his original suit quite out of the question—enveloped in a huge cavalry overcoat (when it is cold) of the same color and texture of the pants; and when the identical flannel blouse worn at Portland—cap with an immense rent in it, caused by a picket raid when we were after Stuart's cavalry, a shawl and rubber talma strapped on behind the saddle and the overcoat (perhaps), or the dressing cases, before—two pistols in holsters, sword about three feet long at side—a piece of blue beef and some hard bread in the saddlebags. This figure seated on a magnificent horse gives that peculiar point and quality of incongruity which constitutes the ludicrous.*

Up until shortly before the battle, he described himself as having a full beard which he then had trimmed into his famous waxed mustache.

PRIVATE COLLECTION

Confederate North Carolina Cavalryman.

A horse takes a roll during a modeling session.

CLEAR THE WAY

The men of the Brig. Gen. Thomas Francis Meagher's Irish Brigade knew it was a suicidal assault. But they were not about to run from a fight. The green banners under which they had fought on the Peninsula and in the Maryland campaign carried the defiant Gaelic words "*Riamh Nar dhruid O sbairn lann*" ("Never retreat from the clash of spears") General Meagher moved among the men in the streets of Fredericksburg as they prepared for the assault, reminding them of their heritage as Sons of Erin and their duty to their adopted country. He ordered all the men to put sprigs of boxwood in their caps to identify themselves as members of the brigade and remind them of the land of their birth.

When they deployed into battle lines on December 13, 1862, the 28th Massachusetts took the center position, with the 116th Pennsylvania and 63rd New York on their left and the 88th and the 69th New York on the right. The Bay Staters held the center of the line because theirs was the only regiment bearing a green flag that day, for the tattered remnants of the New York regiments' flags had been sent home and their replacements had not yet arrived. Their motto was "*Faugh-a-Ballagh*," or "Clear the way," but at Fredericksburg, the way could not be cleared.

The troops emerged from the city "in glorious style," said a soldier from the 8th Ohio Infantry who looked on, "their green sunbursts waving, as they waved on many a bloody battlefield before, in the thick of the fight where the grim and thankless butchery of war is done." Above the thunder of the guns, they heard the fateful words: "Irish Brigade Advance! Forward, double quick, guide center." And through the cornfield they came, though many nourished it with their blood. They passed the first fence and struggled to close up the yawning gaps in their ranks that Confederate lead was constantly opening. Still, they pushed forward to the second fence, within sixty yards of the enemy's batteries. Braving the last small crest in the open plain before the stone wall, they were fully exposed to every Confederate gun on the field. They had entered a slaughterhouse, and even the most determined could do no more than doggedly throw themselves down and fire from among the dead and dying in an attempt to hold the ground they had taken.

It was little consolation that burial parties after the battle reported that the bodies lying closest to the wall all had sprigs of green in their caps. When General Meagher called the brigade to arms on the morning of December 14, only 280 men appeared of the more than 1,300 he had taken into battle the day before. The desperate courage of the Irish had left the brigade a pitiful remnant of the fighting force it had been, but it had gained them a lasting reputation for extraordinary valor, even among their Confederate adversaries. Gen. George Pickett, who would one day lead his own glorious but futile charge, spoke for many Southerners when he wrote to his wife that his "heart almost stood still as I watched those sons of Erin fearlessly rush to their deaths. The brilliant assault was beyond description. Why my darling, we forgot they were fighting us, and cheer after cheer at their fearlessness went up all along our lines."

LAWRENCE F. KOHL

ARTIST COMMENTS

When working on this painting, I was concerned that the strong images of the dead and wounded might cause the print to be unpopular, as gallery owners feared that the scene would be too graphic. I could not think of a way around this, however, and cutting down on the casualties would lessen the sense of danger to the brave Irishmen. So I pitched in without letting the worriers influence my treatment of the subject, and subsequently this became one of my most popular works. The most difficult part of this painting was creating the town of Fredericksburg in the background. Some of the buildings have been altered in appearance since 1862, and it was important to depict them properly. One of the town steeples is presently covered in stucco, but at the time of the battle, it was bare brick.

EVE OF THE STORM

On the morning of May 1, 1863, Generals Robert E. Lee and Thomas J. "Stonewall" Jackson faced daunting odds and tremendous disadvantages in position. Outnumbered by about 130,000 to 60,000—the worst disproportion Lee encountered until the war's final weeks—and outflanked by Union general Joseph Hooker's clever opening gambit, the Southern chieftains contemplated an array of options ranging from dangerous to desperate. Amazingly, they did not shrink from the challenge and retire southward to start the martial minuet anew. Instead, the Confederates moved west from Fredericksburg in the direction of Hooker's concentration at the Chancellorsville crossroads, in the midst of the Wilderness. Hooker recoiled in the face of that audacity and by sunset on May 1 had fallen all the way back to Chancellorsville.

Lee and Jackson conferred that evening a mile south of Hooker's intersection, where the Orange Plank Road crossed the Catharine Furnace Road. Their successful advance on May 1 had improved the Southerners' prospects, but only marginally. The odds remained just as long, and the options almost as limited. Allowing the Northern host to regain the initiative probably would be deadly. How could Lee and Jackson get at Hooker and defeat him? While staff officers hovered at a discreet distance, the two men sat on empty hardtack boxes around a small fire in the cool night, as intelligence seeped in about the enemy position and the roads that might be used to advantage. Gen. A. P. Hill joined them for a time.

Earlier on May 1, Lee had considered the notion of advancing his right against the enemy left, near the Rappahannock River. The Federals lurked there in great strength, a single poor road led into that quadrant of the field, and difficult terrain cut by ridges and streams favored the defense. What about attacking toward the center of the Yankee line at Chancellorsville? The generals sent forward their engineer officers to examine

the ground. Maj. T. M. R. Talcott of Lee's staff and Capt. J. Keith Boswell of Jackson's came back from their moonlit reconnaissance to report the enemy in great strength and entrenching. The situation, Talcott said, "was not favorable to an attack in front." That left only the hope that some means might be uncovered to move secretly across the face of the Northern army and launch a surprise attack against the enemy's far-right flank.

Through that May evening and night, information filtered in about a set of woods paths that might serve the purpose. The reliable Gen. Jeb Stuart scouted in that direction, as did Fitzhugh Lee and Jed Hotchkiss. Rev. Beverley Tucker Lacy, whose brother owned a house in the Wilderness, supplied some details, and civilian women fleeing across the lines added more. By morning, Lee had reached a decision: He would send Jackson on a daring march all the way around the Northern army. The idea was the most dramatic Lee ever hatched, and it led to his greatest victory. When Jackson rode away to execute the plan, he and Lee parted for the last time.

ROBERT K. KRICK

ARTIST COMMENTS

The models for this were all posed in my garage with the doors and windows closed off. For the campfire source of light, a large bulb appropriately positioned on the floor was used to cast an upward light onto the models. Lighting like this must be applied carefully so as not to create an "evil" connotation as one might see in a horror film, where a sinister unnatural upward light is almost always used on the villain's face. The other issue was how dark the scene should be. Some artists prefer to paint a night scene very light, almost as though a blue filter were put over a daytime scene, with everything clearly visible but somewhat toned down. I prefer to paint night scenes very dark, especially when set in the woods, where there is a maze of dark, gloomy shapes and outlines. When I have been in the woods at night, I could hardly see anything at all. Thus, I chose to do this painting with extremely contrasting lights and darks.

Models posing in Stamford parking lot, circa 1982.

Colorbearer, 28th Virginia Infantry.

BEFORE THE STORM

On Saturday afternoon, May 2, 1863, at 5:15 P.M., the Army of Northern Virginia stood on the brink of its greatest triumph. Nearly 30,000 Southern soldiers had followed Stonewall Jackson on a risky secret movement that took them entirely across the face of an enemy force that outnumbered them by a huge margin. An aide to Gen. Jeb Stuart who delivered a message to Jackson along the route found him "ahead of his infantry," looking like "a Deacon on his way to church."

All of Jackson's men marched more than a dozen miles; some covered fifteen. For three hours, the troops arrived steadily at the point of attack, four abreast, turning off the Orange Turnpike to form a carefully concealed line two miles long. North Carolina brigades anchored the formation on both ends, with one brigade each from Alabama and Georgia in the middle, astride the turnpike. The terrain helped maintain secrecy: An Alabamian described "tangled brushwood" so dense that he could see "scarcely ten paces" ahead. The covert line, hidden from Federal view, led a disoriented Virginia captain to tell his men that "there was not a yankee within 5 miles of us."

The Federal XI Corps, commanded by Gen. O. O. Howard, occupied the turnpike on the far right flank of Gen. Joseph Hooker's Army of the Potomac, facing south. Jackson carefully, clandestinely, formed his line perpendicular to Howard's doomed force. He had achieved the field-army equivalent of the classic naval maneuver known as crossing the enemy's T. When Jackson unleashed his men, Northern soldiers would be facing the wrong way by ninety degrees. Only those on the far end of the line could even shoot back. The bravest Yankee in the entire XI Corps could hardly stand for long: Confederates overlapping him by a mile on either side would force him to retreat in short order.

After three nerve-racking hours of preparation, as the final troops filed into their positions, Jackson contemplated what his energy and daring had wrought. His entire corps crouched beyond the flank of an unsuspecting enemy. The brilliant young Maj. Alexander S. "Sandie" Pendleton rode behind Jackson's right shoulder, ready to carry out his chief's dictates. Gen. Robert E. Rodes prepared to launch his troops at the front of Jackson's formation in his first battle as a division commander. Maj. Eugene Blackford of the 5th Alabama, a twenty-four-year-old Fredericksburg native on familiar ground, arranged the screen of skirmishers that shielded the formation and would lead the advance.

Jackson gestured with his hand toward the foe, Blackford reported, and said to Rodes, "Just push them General, push them, all is well." A hero-worshipping Alabama soldier who saw Jackson wave his hand to order Rodes forward thought the Southern legend looked "more like a god than a man" at that electric moment.

Within a few minutes, the screaming Confederates unraveled the enemy flank and sent it scurrying eastward. In the sardonic words of a Federal colonel, the XI Corps "hastily left their position on our right under the influence of an aversion for Stonewall Jackson."

ROBERT K. KRICK

Before the Storm.

ARTIST COMMENTS

This was my first attempt at painting Stonewall, and it has always proven to be the most popular. Although Jackson was usually an austere dresser, his chiseled face and superb nose with his cap drawn down present a powerful, warlike image.

To increase the drama, I isolated Jackson from his staff to emphasize the importance of the decision resting on his shoulders alone. The rubberized raincoat he wore also helped separate him in appearance from the other officers and the background. The dull, earthy tones of Confederate uniforms are often the same colors as the scenery, and it requires careful preparation to make them stand out. When painting the warriors of the South, the artist has to strive to include some colors. Thank goodness that in this case the battle flags were mostly red.

CHARGE!

A t 6:30 P.M. on May 2, 1863, Maj. Pennock Huey led the 8th Pennsylvania Cavalry along a narrow dirt road through the woods leading from Hazel Grove near Chancellorsville toward the Orange Plank Road, with orders to report to the XI Corps. The regiment rode in columns of two, headed by Huey, Maj. Peter Keenan (commander of the regiment's 1st Battalion), Capt. Charles Arrowsmith of Company B, Lt. James E. Carpenter of Company K, and Adj. J. Haseltine Haddock.

Major Huey knew nothing of Stonewall Jackson's flank attack, and the column rode on, occasionally spying foot soldiers moving through the woods as it neared the plank road. Suddenly Huey realized that these soldiers wore gray, not blue. There was no time or room to turn the column around and retreat. Huey gave the only order that seemed possible: "Draw saber and charge!"

As the charging column reached the Orange Plank Road, Huey saw gray-clad infantry moving to the right toward Chancellorsville, the way toward army headquarters. Another line of infantry was approaching from the west, and Huey's horsemen crashed into this line, sending it flying in all directions. But then a volley at close range cut through the column's head, killing Major Keenan, Captain Arrowsmith, and Adjutant Haddock. The charging column lost momentum and headed off into the woods north of the road, to reassemble later that night.

This little-noted charge had later repercussions. When General Jackson rode off to reconnoiter beyond his lines that night, his party was fired on by nervous Confederate infantry, believing that more Yankee cavalry was coming their way.

DR. RICHARD SAUERS

ARTIST COMMENTS

Rarely depicted in modern cavalry charge paintings are riderless horses, of which there would have been a good number as troopers fell off. These terrified animals had a tendency to stay with the group and the other horses they knew and would continue on in the charge. To stage the one in the painting, a fully equipped but riderless horse at the local stable was run in a circle on a long lead. I was surprised at how wildly the stirrups flailed about, something I would not have thought of in the studio. Because no one was controlling the reins, the horse's head was more outstretched during the gallop.

Current renderings rarely depict the proper way for a trumpet to be worn when not in use, slung across the bugler's back, where the lightweight copper instrument would not be damaged or crushed. The buckles on the carbine slings also were worn on the back, where they would not catch on sleeves or reins. Contemporary artists have been misled by period portrait photographs, for which the big brass buckle was placed in front.

Mounted model at full gallop.

JACKSON'S FLANK ATTACK

Late on the afternoon of Saturday, May 2, 1863, nearly 30,000 Confederates under the command of Gen. Stonewall Jackson stood poised to strike the exposed flank of the Union army west of Chancellorsville. A risky clandestine march had taken the men most of the day to cover a dozen miles, but now they were prepared to unleash a violent attack on an unsuspecting enemy. Their line extended for nearly two miles, perpendicular to the Orange Turnpike and squarely on the unsupported right end of the Federal line.

Thickly overgrown country offered plenty of cover for the Southern troops as they made stealthy preparations. One of them recalled the position as a "place where the flowers almost refuse to bloom, and where the birds are scarcely ever heard to sing."

The battle-tested veterans of the 4th Georgia Infantry of Brig. Gen. George P. Doles's brigade anchored their left flank in dense thickets on the turnpike, near the middle of Jackson's attack formation. Doles, thirty-two years old, had entered Confederate service without military training or battle experience, but he turned his four Georgia regiments into a sturdy unit. After Doles was killed the following spring, his widow described her husband as five feet, ten and a half inches tall, 145 to 150 pounds, with blue eyes and brown hair.

By the time the alignment satisfied Stonewall Jackson's exacting standards, the sun was slanting down toward the western horizon. When Stonewall said quietly to division commander Robert E. Rodes, "You can go forward then," the Army of Northern Virginia's greatest moment had arrived. This most famous of Jackson's attacks would also be his last.

As they moved forward, thousands of Southern soldiers advancing in close alignment through the thickets drove forest creatures in front of them, rather like beaters driving game on an African safari. Animals and birds scurried eastward, away from the thick bands of humans moving steadily through the brush. The wildlife gave many Union soldiers of the

37th New York, Irish Rifles.

XI Corps the first hint of their impending doom. Gen. O. O. Howard, commanding the corps, described the phenomenon: "Its first lively effects, like a cloud of dust driven before a coming storm, appeared in the startled rabbits, squirrels, quail and other game flying wildly hither and thither in evident terror, and escaping where possible into adjacent clearings." A Confederate advancing just to Doles's left recalled that "the Yankees . . . were surprised alright, for the first intimation they had of the approach of our troops was the rabbits and foxes running into where they were cooking."

Many overwhelmed Federals "fled before us equal to sheep," reported Col. Charles F. Morse, but some found positions from which to fight back. When the Confederate tide faltered at a line of works, "Gen. Doles riding up and down the line at this moment soon rallied the men," said Morse, "and dashing forward we drove the Yankees from the breastworks."

The stunning Confederate onslaught shattered the XI Corps. In the droll words of a Federal colonel's official report, that corps "hastily left their position on our right under the influence of an aversion for Stonewall Jackson."

ROBERT K. KRICK

ARTIST COMMENTS

Lighting of this sort is always challenging for any painter, and a lifelike quality can be elusive. The results when successful create a most powerful and dramatic effect on the viewer. This is not artwork that can be thrown together by posing models in a studio or open area, and then just painting them among some trees. A studio painting can often be detected by the lack of strong lighting or shadows on the figures. The end result is grayish, muted tones even in what should be bright daylight. Many nineteenth-century artists posed their models under a frosted glass skylight so the natural lighting each day would always be consistent. The finished works produced by this means appear to have been painted on an overcast day.

Artists that work from what is known in the trade as "scrap," assorted pictures clipped from magazines and old books taken under various lighting conditions have to tone down the strong lighting in order to combine all of this diversely lit material. Giving myself every opportunity to shape this painting into a credible image, I posed all of the models on-site in the deep woods very late in the day. Not much light at all filtered through the leaves, and in some areas almost none.

Irish recruiting poster.
TROIANI COLLECTION

BRANDY STATION REVIEW

Gen. "Jeb" Stuart loved color and show and noise and flair. His enthusiasm for the impressive panoply afforded by a grand review led to a famous display of mounted Confederate military might near Brandy Station on June 8, 1863.

The general had reviewed his cavalry with considerable pomp and circumstance on June 5 and decided to reprise the gaudy event on the eighth when the army's commanding general, R. E. Lee, agreed to participate. Some enlisted cavalrymen grumbled about the useless exertion but "ceased in a measure when it was learned that Genl. Robert E. Lee was to be present and witness the review."

Trooper Robert Hudgins of the 3rd Virginia Cavalry prepared for the gala day by grooming his horse "as slick as a peeled onion" and shining his gear until his "spurs and accoutrements sparkled in the sun like a mirror." Hudgins and his mates heard that Lee would be on hand, "and you can bet your boots that each of us was on our best behavior," he recalled.

On June 8, some 8,000 cavalrymen marshaled on the review grounds along the Orange and Alexandria Railroad not far east of Culpeper Court House, Virginia. The familiar figure of the army's much-loved commander rode into view soon after noon. Lee brought with him his chief of artillery, Gen. William Nelson Pendleton. The artillerist's dignified, gray-haired visage did not adorn the soul of a skilled warrior, but it led some civilians to confuse him with General Lee. Stuart and his cavalcade of bright young staff officers swung into ranks behind Lee, and the whole entourage set off at a gallop down the carefully aligned ranks. One of Stuart's lieutenants described the cavalier at this moment, riding joyfully in the midst of his element: "Ardent, full of life, the dark cavalry feather, the lofty forehead, and dazzling blue eyes. . . . His boots reached to the knees; a yellow silk sash wound about his waist."

The front stretched nearly a mile across a bare, grassy plain. Most of the reviewers thundered across the ground at a rapid clip. Lee had only a few years before been commanding cavalry on the vast Texan frontier, and a few thousand yards across Virginia's fertile late-spring fields hardly affected the seasoned horseman. General Pendleton was a much less experienced horseman from a cloistered clerical background, however, and quickly fell behind. Unfazed by the jostling from his hard ride, Parson Pendleton reported to his wife with gusto, "A grand show it was." "Never had the plains of Culpeper witnessed a spectacle more magnificent," a Virginia cavalryman wrote. "For once war seemed turned to carnival; and flowers wreathed the keen edge of the sword." The presence of women in the appreciative audience added to the festive aspect for the horse soldiers, who had long been exiled from civilization's gentler influences.

Before twenty-four hours passed, the troopers who had eagerly flourished polished swords as General Lee rode past would be wielding their weapons in earnest in the battle of Brandy Station, fought over ground adjacent to the review site.

ROBERT K. KRICK

ARTIST COMMENTS

I concentrated heavily on the appearance of Lee and his staff, incorporating all known descriptions of their dress and

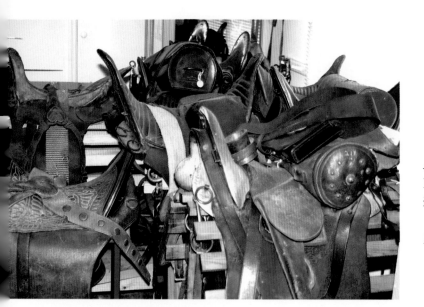

Part of the original cavalry horse equipage collection.

LARRY PAGE

equipage. Contrary to many portrayals, Stuart often wore his jacket buttoned across when in the field, and the jacket was solid gray and did not have yellow lapels as frequently shown. Of particular interest was the large silver badge and chain ornament he wore fastened to his chest, described by a Union prisoner who met him about that time. Horse equipage has always been a strong study area, and it lends a solid credibility to the subject when done properly.

THE GRAY COMANCHES

Six companies of tough, lean, graceful horsemen from Virginia's Shenandoah Valley and the adjacent Piedmont region went to war in 1861 to fight Yankees. The Confederate government designated the unit the 35th Virginia Cavalry Battalion. But because of the men's flair and style, as well as the savage shrieks they unleashed when charging, the battalion came to be known universally as the Comanches.

The Comanches suffered their heaviest losses of the war in winning perhaps their most dramatic triumph at a moment of crisis during the cavalry cataclysm at Brandy Station on June 9, 1863. A surprising Federal onset early that morning launched a day of chaotic fighting that swirled across a stretch of rolling meadows east of Culpeper Court House, Virginia. Mounted men adept at reconnaissance and screening, in the traditional role of nineteenth-century cavalry, fought on this day dismounted like infantry or galloped recklessly forward in thunderous assaults.

The importance of a ridge called Fleetwood Hill soon became apparent to both sides. The ridge's crest commanded a wide arc in every direction. Squadrons fought bitter encounters on Fleetwood's grassy slopes as control of the high ground teetered precariously in the balance. Late in the morning, Gen. Jeb Stuart sent his renowned Laurel Brigade, which included the Comanches, to Fleetwood in an effort to turn the tide. The battalion's thirty-year-old commander, Lt. Col. Elijah Viers White, led his men in the race for the hilltop. Federal reinforcements threatened "Lije" White's men and their fellow Virginia troopers from a dangerous flank, and artillery fire flailed their line.

The colonel spun his battalion toward the hostile artillery and ordered the men to follow him in a charge into the teeth of the guns. Screaming gray-clad horsemen, waving swords and pistols, spurred their mounts forward in a desperate dash. The Northern gunners, who belonged to Capt. Joseph W. Martin's New York Battery, hurled lead and iron into the ranks of the Confederates galloping straight into the battery's position. One of the Virginians recalled a "perfect storm" of canister and a "rain of bullets" that scythed through the battalion. An onlooker watched and marveled: "Could they live under such a fire? The smoke partly obscured the issue, but through the rifts were seen the charging horsemen bearing down upon the foe." The Northern gunners, a Comanche wrote admiringly, "fought like heroes, with small arms, long after their guns were silenced. There was no demand for a surrender, nor any offer to do so."

Captain Martin lost three artillery pieces but boasted of his cannoneers' bravery: "Of the little band who defended the battery not one of them flinched for a moment from his duty." When he mustered his fragmented remnants that night, Martin reported twenty-one of thirty-six killed, wounded, or missing. Their stirring feat of arms cost the Comanches at least ninety casualties. The battalion's historian bragged of two flags captured, more than 100 prisoners taken, and much booty in horses and equipment, "but," he concluded dolefully, "many of its gallant men had been lost."

ROBERT K. KRICK

ARTIST COMMENTS

A perennial dilemma in research is ascertaining the color of the horse a particular individual rode. A writer can simply say, "Captain So-and-So rode up to the general and said . . . ," but the painter must show the captain's horse in color. Often this can present a huge obstacle to the dedicated historical painter. Invariably the information is recorded somewhere, but digging it out can be an almost insurmountable task on occasion. In White's papers in the National Archives, Jerry Coates found a receipt for his horse killed at Brandy Station—a gray. A rare stroke of luck.

McPherson's Ridge

At 11 A.M. on June 30, 1863, 2,900 weary Federal cavalrymen rode into the town of Gettysburg. Organized into two brigades, these troopers were led by Brig. Gen. John Buford, their division commander. Buford, known as "Old Steadfast," was a thirty-six-year-old West Pointer who had seen many years of hard service in the West before the Civil War.

Arriving in the town, Buford, with a veteran's trained eye for terrain, recognized the strong defensive features of McPherson's Ridge. He then set about designing a defense in depth to the north and west of the town, where Confederate infantry was known to be massing along the Chambersburg Pike. He deployed the brigade of Col. William Gamble of the 8th Illinois Cavalry along either side of the Chambersburg Pike and the brigade of Col. Thomas C. Devin of the 6th New York Cavalry to the north and east of the town. Buford also brought up Battery A, 2nd U.S. Artillery, commanded by Lt. John Calef, a fine, young horse artillerist. Setting up vedette posts well to the west of McPherson's Ridge, Buford established an effective early-warning system. That night, Buford held a council of war with Devin, Gamble, Calef, and his staff, wherein the next day's plans were discussed. Tom Devin, always spoiling for a fight, announced that he would hold his position the next day. But Buford, ever the realist, told Devin: "No, you won't. They will attack you in the morning and they will come booming—skirmishers three deep."

At about 5 A.M. on July 1, Lt. Marcellus E. Jones squeezed off a shot at the advancing Confederate infantry. The infantry stopped to form a line of battle, and nearly two hours passed before it resumed its steady approach. Engaging Buford's troopers on Herr's Ridge, about a mile to the west of McPherson's Ridge, the blue-clad horsemen held off the gray-clad infantry for nearly an hour. Finally, the sheer weight of the Confederate numbers forced the Federals back to McPherson's Ridge, where their resistance stiffened.

Buford, accompanied only by his bugler, rode his lines atop his magnificent Thoroughbred warhorse, Grey Eagle. Meeting Calef as the young artillerist brought his guns to the field, Buford instructed him to deploy his three sections on a wide front to create the illusion that he had more artillery support. Calef deployed one section on either side of the road near the McPherson barn and another section about 800 yards away. His guns opened on the Confederates, and soon a fierce counterbattery duel erupted.

At 9:30, just as the Federal horsemen were running out of ammunition, the Army of the Potomac's infantry arrived on the field and saved the day. Later, John Buford proudly wrote: "The zeal, bravery, and good behavior of the officers and men on the night of June 30, and during July 1, was commendable in the extreme. A heavy task was before us; we were equal to it, and shall all remember with pride that at Gettysburg we did our country much service."

ERIC J. WITTENBURG

ARTIST COMMENTS

Correctly portraying the artillery harness here was particularly perplexing, as there is some confusion about how exactly some of the straps connecting the horses were set up. I have a good bit of original artillery harness in my collection, allowing me to have it by the easel while working. Many modern renderings of artillery harness depict it as much too dainty and skimpy. My research showed that the drivers would usually lay the whip across the horse's back and then just give it a flick, rather than dramatically lashing as seen in many paintings. I worked with historian Kathy George of Gettysburg National Park on reconstructing the appearance of the McPherson farm, and she was of invaluable assistance.

Artillery saddle, valise, and saddle blanket.

TROIANI COLLECTION

McPherson's Ridge.

A sketch of the barn done a year or two after the battle by Pvt. Robert Knox Sneden of the 40th New York Volunteers was also handy. For some reason this important sketch was not published in either of the compilations of this soldier-artist's amazing work, *Eye of the Storm* or *Images of the Storm*. I had a rare opportunity to photograph many of his original drawings before they were sold to the Virginia Historical Society.

For God's Sake Forward

The baptism of fire for the 2nd Wisconsin Volunteer Infantry happened in July 1861 on the battlefield of First Bull Run. Not present on that battlefield, but no doubt keenly aware of the events, was Lt. Col. John F. Reynolds of the 14th U.S. Infantry. Little did both parties know that in a little less than two years, their actions on the battlefield of Gettysburg would be an indelible part of each other's fate and place in history.

In the midmorning hours of July 1, 1863, the 2nd Wisconsin, now a battle-hardened regiment of the famed Iron Brigade, found itself waiting in the Emmitsburg Road near the Nicholas Codori farm. To the west, the men of the regiment could hear the dull thuds of artillery, an early indication of the pitched battle raging between portions of the division of Maj. Gen. Henry Heth and the dismounted Union troopers of Brig. Gen. John Buford's brigade.

Earlier that morning, after conferring with Buford and surveying the position, Reynolds, now a major general commanding the left wing of the Army of the Potomac, decided to make a stand in the fields west of Gettysburg. Turning to his aide, Capt. Stephen Weid, he dictated what would be his last dispatch to Maj. Gen. George Meade, commanding the Army of the Potomac: "The enemy is advancing in strong force, and I fear he might get to the heights beyond the town before I can. I will fight him inch by inch, and if driven into the town I will barricade the streets and hold him back as long as possible." Not being one to leave things to providence, he soon departed to hurry up the Union infantry.

For the men of the 2nd Wisconsin, their rest was short-lived, as they soon saw Reynolds approach with orders to proceed with all possible haste to support Buford. "Forward, double quick!" was the order as the Iron Brigade left the Emmitsburg Road and proceeded cross-country to the scene of action. With the 2nd Wisconsin leading, and marching in columns of four, the Iron Brigade passed the large Lutheran seminary building. Upon seeing the 2nd Wisconsin crest Seminary Ridge, and not waiting for the rest of the brigade to come up, Reynolds ordered the regiment to move forward into line" and charge into the woods on McPherson's Ridge, all in a desperate attempt to blunt the Confederate advance.

Urging the 2nd Wisconsin on, Reynolds called out, "Forward men, forward for God's sake and drive those fellows out of the woods." Within moments of shouting his encouragement, Reynolds was struck by a minié ball in the back of his neck, never again to regain consciousness. For the 2nd Wisconsin, their work on the battlefield of Gettysburg was just beginning. Of the 300 men who filled the unit's ranks, 182 would be wounded or killed during the three-day battle of Gettysburg.

KEITH KNOKE

ARTIST COMMENTS

Here I attempted to portray a line of battle rushing through the wooded area. I chose this angle so that not only General Reynolds would be visible, but also some of the buildings in the far background. When composing a painting such as this, it is always difficult to include all the interesting terrain features. Whatever angle the artist choses usually eliminates something interesting on the other side.

Projectile damage to trees is something artists often neglect to include in battle paintings. In a heavy fire, the troops underneath trees would be showered with leaves, branches, and bark. There is no substitute for the real thing, so with two .58 Springfield rifle-muskets, a couple of friends and I blasted live rounds into a large tree near my house. I photographed every strike for future reference, and the mystery was solved. The tree died.

Blasting holes in trees with rifled muskets.

Minié ball holes fired into backyard trees in order to see precisely what such damage would look like.

Original piece of fence rail with embedded bullet.

CONNECTICUT MUSEUM OF HISTORY

Generals Robert E. Lee and A. P. Hill,
Gettysburg Campaign, 1863.

"BOY COLONEL"

Fighting on July 1, 1863, rapidly escalated into full-scale combat at Gettysburg. Men of the Union I Corps put up a stiff resistance as the battle-hardened veterans of Maj. Gen. A. P. Hill's Corps of Lee's Army of Northern Virginia strove to dislodge the Federals from the fields and woods west of town. By 2 P.M., the Confederates were poised to renew their assault. Brig. Gen. James J. Pettigrew's brigade anxiously awaited the chance to enter the fray, and the orders finally came to do so.

The largest regiment in the brigade belonged to the 26th North Carolina, containing 926 men. It was led by Col. Henry King Burgwyn Jr., at twenty-one years old the youngest colonel in Lee's army. He came from a distinguished North Carolina family, attended that state's university, and graduated from the Virginia Military Institute. His age was no impediment to his leadership abilities. Burgwyn had led his men since August of the previous year, earning their respect through his hard work, fairness, and attention to detail.

The North Carolinians splashed across Willoughby Run and charged headlong through McPherson's Woods. Their destination was the Union line, manned by the famed Iron Brigade, arrayed along McPherson's Ridge. Directly in front of Burgwyn's men were the infantrymen of the 24th Michigan and the 19th Indiana. The Federals poured a deadly fire into their attackers, and casualties in the Southern regiment quickly mounted.

Hit particularly hard during the charge were the men of the color guard. The color-bearers were shot down, and the regiment's flag fell to the ground. But each time, a brave man picked it up and continued on. When the fighting was particularly severe, Colonel Burgwyn noticed Lt. George Wilcox shot twice trying to move the flag forward. The "boy colonel" quickly snatched the flag from Wilcox and pressed onward, yelling, "Dress on the colors." It was certainly no position for the commander of the regiment to be in, but the brave young officer paid no heed for his personal safety. Finally, Pvt. Frank Honeycutt came forward to carry the flag. As Burgwyn turned to give the flag to him, a bullet ripped into his side, and he fell to the ground. Within two hours, Henry K. Burgwyn Jr. was dead. His last thoughts were for his men and of his family.

JAY JORGENSEN

Confederate wooden canteen captured by Connecticut soldier.

TROIANI COLLECTION

FIGHT FOR THE COLORS

The men of the famed 6th Wisconsin Volunteer Infantry came from small Wisconsin communities such as Fond du Lac, Baraboo, and Prescott. The men of the equally lauded 2nd Mississippi Volunteer Infantry, CSA, came from similar communities in northern Mississippi. Separated by more than 700 miles at the beginning of the war, in the late morning of July 1, 1863, in the fields west of Gettysburg, Pennsylvania, these two veteran regiments would meet face-to-face.

Unlike the other three regiments of the Iron Brigade, who had charged headlong into the woods on McPherson's Ridge in an effort to check the advance of Confederate brigadier general James Archer's brigade, the 6th Wisconsin was held as division reserve in the swale between Seminary Ridge and McPherson's Ridge. The regiment had little time to enjoy their relative safety, however, for the situation on the division's right flank was deteriorating rapidly. The Mississippians and North Carolinians of Brig. Gen. Joseph R. Davis's brigade were driving Brig. Gen. Lysander Cutler's Union brigade back beyond the Chambersburg Pike. In an effort to stabilize his shaken Union right, Maj. Gen. Abner Doubleday ordered the 6th Wisconsin to the right. Wasting little time, Lt. Col. Rufus Dawes of the 6th ordered, "Right Face!" "Double-quick, march!" With little time to spare, the 6th reached the Chambersburg Pike, where they were ordered to fire by file and, momentarily at least, succeeded in halting Davis's advance. Caught by surprise by this unexpected resistance the men of the 42nd Mississippi, 2nd Mississippi, and the 55th North Carolina of Davis's brigade took advantage of the cover at hand and jumped into the cut of an unfinished railroad. Recalling the event years later, one Wisconsin soldier wrote: "I could not help thinking, now, for once, we will have a square stand up and knock down fight. No trees, nor walls to protect either, when presto! their whole line disappeared as if swallowed by the earth."

Unknown head intrudes into reference shot for Fight for the Colors.

Although it was out of the direct line of fire, what little organization Davis's brigade had before entering the cut was now gone. Maj. John Blair of the 2nd Mississippi wrote that "all the men were jumbled together without regard to regiment or company." To complicate matters further, the arrival of the 6th Wisconsin allowed portions of Cutler's brigade to reform on the 6th Wisconsin's left. For Davis, it was apparent that the Confederate advance had stalled and the Union force to his front was about to seize the initiative. Left with few alternatives, Davis ordered a retreat.

Davis was correct in his assessment of the situation, for at that moment, the 6th Wisconsin, 95th New York, and 14th Brooklyn were preparing to charge. "Forward! Forward! Charge!" ordered Dawes. "Align on the Colors! Align on the Colors!" It took just a few moments for the men of the Badger State to cover the 400 feet to the Chambersburg Pike and the railroad cut. For Corp. Frank Waller of the 6th Wisconsin, the charge placed him in a desperate struggle with Color Corp. William B. Murphy of the 2nd Mississippi. At stake was the fiercely protected battle flag of the 2nd Mississippi.

Recalling the struggle years later, Murphy wrote:

My color guards were all killed and wounded in less than five minutes, and also my colors were shot more than one dozen times, and the flag staff was hit and splintered two or three times. Just about that time a squad of soldiers

made a rush for my colors and our men did their duty. They were all killed or wounded, but they still rushed for the colors with one of the most deadly struggles that was ever witnessed during any battle in the war. They still kept rushing for my flag and there were over a dozen shot down like sheep in their mad rush for the colors. The first soldier was shot down just as he made for the flag, and he was shot by one of our soldiers. Just to my right and at the same time a lieutenant made a desperate struggle for the flag and was shot through the right shoulder. Over a dozen men fell killed or wounded, and then a large man made a rush for me and the flag. As I tore the flag from the staff he took hold of me and the color.

Corporals Waller and Murphy both survived the battle of Gettysburg and the war, and Waller received the Medal of Honor for his actions that day. Both men long remembered that struggle near the railroad cut and that fight for the colors.

KEITH KNOKE

ARTIST COMMENTS

This work has become one of my most popular paintings. Perhaps the classic struggle for the colors has come to symbolize the North-South conflict in a nutshell. With the exception of the modern bridge and fence lines, the railroad cut today has changed little from its 1863 appearance. It is

Lutheran Seminary as it is today, near the stand of the 24th Michigan. KATHY GEORGE

easy to see how what was originally perceived as a good, sheltered position by the Confederate troops quickly became a trap. Once the Union troops had crossed the line of fire and arrived at the rim, it became a fishbowl from which the Southern troops could not escape.

Using an exact replica of the 6th Mississippi flag borrowed from flag historian Howard Madaus, I spent quite a while working with the models to achieve a realistic grapple. Only when they actually tried to tear the flag from each other's grasp did a credible scenario arise. Whenever possible, the models were urged to actually struggle with each other, sometimes to the point of where I had to intervene when they began to take it too seriously. It also was sometimes necessary to exaggerate the poses in order to increase the sense of drama and action. The wounded officer on the left of the painting is renowned marine artist Chris Blossom, who agreed to pose that day. Artists always make great models, as they know exactly what is needed.

Federal infantry Hardee hat worn by the Iron Brigade.
TROIANI COLLECTION

Iron Brigade

Composed of six to eight corporals and a sergeant, the color guard of a regiment of infantry in the Civil War held a position of honor and high regard. For the color guard of the 24th Michigan Volunteer Infantry, the pride they felt at being part of this trusted few may have been surpassed only by the pride they felt at belonging to the famed Iron Brigade.

The Virginia-born Col. Henry Morrow of the 24th Michigan entrusted the regimental colors to a forty-two-year-old farmer, Color Sgt. Able Peck. He and the rest of the 24th had spent the early morning of July 1, 1863, preparing for a battle that now seemed all but inevitable. By 6:30 that morning, the regiment had left its position along Marsh Creek, to begin a six-mile march to Gettysburg. Reaching the fields west of town, the 24th Michigan, along with the rest of the Iron Brigade, was hastily formed and deployed in an effort to check the Confederate advance.

Being the leftmost regiment of the brigade, the 24th advanced, only to find their line extended beyond the right flank of Brig. Gen. James Archer's Confederate brigade. Not being one to miss an opportunity, Colonel Morrow ordered the regiment to envelop the Confederate right. Although successful in driving the Confederates from their position, the movement resulted in the loss of Color Sergeant Peck to a wound in the head. He would be the first of seven bearers killed or wounded that day.

Reacting quickly, Color Corp. Charles Bellore grabbed the colors from Peck's hands before they touched the ground. Bellore had the honor of carrying the flag for only short period of time before he, too, was killed during the regiment's stand on McPherson's Ridge. With the colors now in the hands of Color Corp. August Earnest, the weight of the Confederate advance forced the Iron Brigade back toward Seminary Ridge. Like those who preceded him, Earnest spent his final moments holding the colors aloft. Two more color bearers fell mortally wounded, while carrying the flag on the retreat to the regiment's rallying point near the crest of Seminary Ridge.

Upon reaching the crest, and desperate to rally what was left of his regiment, Colonel Morrow grabbed the flag, holding it aloft and shouting, "Rally!" But like those before him, Morrow was shot down soon after raising the colors. The regiment made one more desperate but short-lived stand near the seminary buildings but soon were compelled to join in the retreat of the Union forces through town. Unlike many of those who carried the regiment's colors that day, Colonel Morrow lived to fight another day.

Keith Knoke

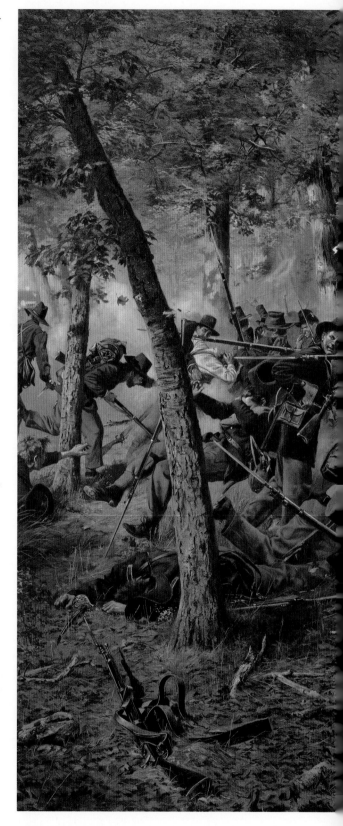

ARTIST COMMENTS

I am often asked why the men of the 24th Michigan are not wearing the well-known white leggings associated with the Iron Brigade. The 24th joined the brigade well after the leggings had been issued to the original units and therefore never had any. By the time of Gettysburg, there probably were not too many pairs remaining in the brigade.

WALTER WALPIN

At 52 by 80 inches, this is a huge painting, and difficulties arose when I initially sketched in the figures, as my studio did not allow me enough room to step back and view the canvas from a distance. Eighteenth-century painters dealt with this problem by using brushes several feet long.

Although I prefer to work on a board, which has a smooth surface that allows for greater detail, large pieces must be on stretched canvas because of weight considerations. This is the largest size I can do, as anything longer will not fit down my studio stairs.

CEMETERY HILL

On July 1, 1863, the newly appointed Union army commander, Gen. George Gordon Meade, along with his II Corps leader, Gen. Winfield Scott Hancock, arrived in Taneytown, Maryland. There, Meade met with his deputy and shared his thoughts about the impending battle he thought might occur at Pipe's Creek. When Meade soon learned that his celebrated wing commander, Gen. John Reynolds, had been killed, he immediately knew that his replacement would be Gen. Oliver Otis Howard of the XI Corps, a man who did not know his intentions or desires. Reynolds's regrettable death now dictated that Meade have an on-site officer who knew and understood his wishes to guide any unfolding events accordingly in that small Pennsylvania town of Gettysburg, thirteen miles to the north.

Reaching out to the Keystone native who had been placed in charge of the II Corps only about five weeks earlier, Meade ordered General Hancock to go to Gettysburg and assume command of the field. Hancock was also directed to determine whether Gettysburg would be a good place to do battle with Robert E. Lee's army. "Make an examination of the ground . . . and report [back] to me," Meade instructed.

Shortly after 1:00 P.M., after turning command of his II Corps to Gen. John Gibbon, the 2nd Division executive, Hancock climbed into an ambulance with a few aides, his horse following, and headed for Gettysburg. Arriving at Cemetery Hill around 4 P.M., Hancock began supervising the disheartened army. It was noted that "his arrival alone, at that critical moment, was like the reenforcement of an army corps." Testy moments must have arisen as the mounted Hancock firmly gave directives to Gen. Abner Doubleday, commander of the 1st Division, XI Corps, while General Howard suffered from Meade's ignominious directive that a subordinate, Hancock, could usurp his superior authority on that field. Unknown to Howard, General Meade had been given congressional authority to make such an unusual appointment. This temperamental encounter gave rise to the disputed rivalry known as the Hancock–Howard controversy. Hancock himself recorded that "it was not a very agreeable office," but he had been a soldier longer than Howard, and General Meade's orders were to be followed.

A. M. GAMBONE

ARTIST COMMENTS

Several superb images of the Evergreen Cemetery gatehouse were taken just after the battle. Black and white photos tell only part of the story in most cases, and the artist must endeavor to seek out the remaining truth. It was popular in the nineteenth century for brick buildings to be painted brown or red-brown rather than leave the bare brick finish. Close study of the photos revealed that the gatehouse was indeed painted. Artist Donna Neary already had closely examined the building, finding traces of the original brown paint still extant in crevices, and generously shared her data with me.

To my knowledge, Hancock's actual horse equipage has not survived, so I used a unique original set from my collection as a model. I was later amused to see that other artists had copied this equipage from my painting, apparently finding it easiest to use my work for reference. Quite a compliment!

Private, 45th New York Infantry, July 1863.

PRIVATE COLLECTION

DECISION AT DAWN

By any imaginable gauge, the fighting around Gettysburg, Pennsylvania, on July 1, 1863, must be adjudged one of the most successful days in the history of Gen. Robert E. Lee's Army of Northern Virginia. Confederate columns concentrating toward the crossroads at Gettysburg on several azimuths had fallen on exposed Federal flanks, at least as much the result of good fortune as of good planning. Southern momentum had dissipated late on July 1, as inexperienced commanders equivocated instead of continuing to ride the roaring tide of success their troops had generated.

Early on July 2, at his headquarters near Gettysburg's Lutheran Seminary, Lee deliberated on the options available to him as he sought to extend the initial triumph. Much of the army's high command had gathered around the general, joined by a sizable detachment of foreign observers. Behind John Bell Hood's tawny beard and lugubrious countenance lurked the spirit of a warrior, but he had no excess of acuity. A. P. Hill, facing his first battle as a corps commander, was destined to be mysteriously invisible all weekend long. Hill's subordinate Harry Heth, who had survived a bullet bouncing off his head the day before—and the only man in the entire army, it was said, whom Lee addressed by his given name—accompanied his chief. James Longstreet, Lee's highest-ranking subordinate, whittled on a stick in ill humor; the army commander, it was becoming apparent, intended to retain the initiative, and Longstreet had never felt comfortable in that role.

Four foreigners, among the most renowned of the numerous Europeans who had come across the Atlantic to observe the American war, looked on as Lee contemplated the day's operations. Each left extensive and historically valuable accounts of what they saw. Lt. Col. A. J. L. Fremantle of the British Army, outfitted in civilian attire and a tall top hat, climbed a nearby tree for a better view. Capt. Justus Scheibert of the Prussian Army perched on an adjacent limb, from which he wrote, "the battlefield lay before us like a panorama." Austrian captain FitzGerald Ross, his mustache groomed "as beautifully as if he was on parade at Vienna," was dressed in an immaculate blue uniform with gold piping. Francis C. Lawley, correspondent for the *London Times*, had been too ill to ride a horse for several days but turned up to make notes on this momentous occasion. The English journalist thought that Lee seemed "more anxious and ruffled than I had ever seen him before, though it required close observation to detect it." Through a field glass, Ross observed that "there was a full view of the enemy's position . . . near enough for us to distinguish every individual figure." The Austrian remained a Confederate enthusiast the rest of his life, describing in 1864 to Jeb Stuart "how fervently I pray for your success. May it come speedily too."

From this morning conference, Lee dispatched Longstreet on a long march to the Confederate right, where fierce fighting ensued at the Peach Orchard, the Wheatfield, and the Round Tops.

ROBERT K. KRICK

ARTIST COMMENTS

For decades, I've accumulated every description I could find of each important general of the war. I keep copies of all these documents, including obscure eyewitness accounts, in individual file folders. Over time, I've created a resource archive of how these individuals appeared over the course of the war. For this painting, the materials in my file drawers allowed me to recreate the crucial scene.

Foreign observers' accounts are often the most helpful, as they frequently comment on articles of dress and other trivial details that American chroniclers rarely bothered to mention. Col. Arthur Freemantle of the Coldstream Guards, a visitor to Lee's headquarters during the Gettysburg campaign, provided in his commentaries a bounty of detail not found elsewhere. An Austrian military observer with Lee's staff that morning was Capt. FitzGerald Ross. Desiring to depict him accurately, I established that he was in the 6th Regiment of Hussars, and then studied that regiment's uniform details.

Decision at Dawn.

"THE MEN MUST SEE US TODAY"

Late on the afternoon of July 2, 1863, Robert E. Lee launched a furious attack against the Union left flank. Gen. James Longstreet referred to the ensuing fighting as "the best three hours' fighting ever done by any troops on any battle-field." At the outset of the fighting there was intense action at Devil's Den. Brig. Gen. Jerome Robertson's Texas Brigade assaulted the Union line atop Houck's Ridge, commanded by Brig. Gen. J. H. Hobart Ward. The Union position was anchored on the left by Capt. James Smith's New York Battery of four Parrotts. To the right of the cannons was the 124th New York Infantry Regiment, led by Col. Augustus Van Horne Ellis.

The New Yorkers had been mustered into service in the fall of 1862 but had seen little combat until May 1863. Hailing from Orange County, the men wore orange ribbons in their buttonholes as reminders of home. At Chancellorsville, as Colonel Ellis urged his men onward, he referred to them as his "Orange Blossoms," a nickname that stuck. During the battle of Chancellorsville, they saw plenty of action, suffering a 40 percent casualty rate. By Gettysburg, only 18 officers and 220 men were left in the regiment.

Colonel Ellis was a hard-fighting, hard-living man. A prewar lawyer, Ellis came from a well-known family. He sought his fame and fortune in the California gold rush. When that did not pan out, he tried his hand at selling real estate and working at sea. Now, as the Texans began their assault at Gettysburg, Ellis stood behind the center of his line and calmly awaited the enemy. Twice Maj. James Cromwell pleaded with Colonel Ellis to order a charge, but both times Ellis refused.

Finally, as the two foes were about to become entangled in combat, Colonel Ellis ordered the officers' horses brought forward. He quickly mounted and prepared for a charge. Capt. William Silliman protested, asserting that mounted officers would be conspicuous targets under the circumstances. Ellis simply replied, "The men must see us today." Indeed, the colonel gave the command to his men to charge into the Texans. Maj. James Cromwell led the assault, and the Orange Blossoms swept the Confederates back through the triangular field. Soon thereafter, Cromwell took a bullet in the chest and died. Seeing Cromwell fall, Colonel Ellis shouted: "My God! My God! Your major's down; save him! Save him!" Unfortunately, those would be his last words of command, for he too was killed while mounted on his horse. The men of the 124th New York carried the bodies of their two fallen officers, Cromwell and Ellis, from the field.

JAY JORGENSEN

Jerry Coates's daughter Hope during a shoot at Devil's Den.

ARTIST COMMENTS

Taking a break from the collector show in Gettysburg, Paul Loane, Earl J. Coates, Jan Gordon, and I met with historian Kathy George to survey the ground at Devil's Den, where the 124th New York had made its stand. Today, there is heavy tree cover, but in 1863, much of the rocky hillock was bare, so the pictures taken that day were not too helpful. I had to return in the fall after the leaves were down in order to get better pictures showing the lay of the land.

53rd Georgia Infantry, 1863.

SAVING THE FLAG

When Gen. Daniel Sickles moved his III Corps into a new position in the prenoon hours of July 2, 1863, the field was still lush and cattle casually grazed on the cool grass in the small pasture at its lower end. This was one of the weakest parts of the Union battle line, protected only by a battery of guns from Winslow's New York Artillery and a very thin line of skirmishers and sharpshooters. When the Confederate Army of Northern Virginia launched its attack against the Union left at about 4 P.M., the noticeable gap in the Union line was quickly observed and just as quickly filled. Forces from other parts of the line held by the Union Army of the Potomac were rushed to the new front, reaching their destination just in time.

The battle here opened when parts of the brigades of Generals George Anderson and Joseph Kershaw descended from the wooded ridge between the Rose Farm buildings and the Wheatfield. Col. Jacob Sweitzer's brigade of the Union V Corps was ordered into the Wheatfield from its position along the public road at its northern edge to support this successful attack across the field of trampled grain and into the woods. Three regiments advanced in line, with the 4th Michigan Volunteers on its right flank. Before they were fairly across the field, however, the tables had turned.

Wofford's brigade of Georgians, originally ordered to follow the brigade of Barksdale at the Peach Orchard, had moved instead into the Loop and the woods along the western edge of the Wheatfield. Here they drove the last remnant of Union forces from the salient of the new Union line, and the men of the Irish Brigade fled to the safety of Cemetery Ridge through the guns of Winslow's battery. Colonel Sweitzer believed these fleeing units had been relieved by other V Corps infantrymen and did not suspect that Confederates now occupied the woods, even after several shots fell among his men from that direction. Believing that these were gunshots from Union forces attempting to fire over and beyond Sweitzer and into the woods at Anderson's

Working on "Saving the Flag" in the studio.

Photos of the Wheatfield taped together for "Saving the Flag."

Georgians, the brigade continued on, deeper into the lowest part of the Wheatfield. A soldier remarked to an astonished Sweitzer, "Colonel, I'll be damned if I don't think we are faced the wrong way; the rebs are up there in the woods behind us, on the right." As if to verify it, men of the 4th Michigan began to fall, with balls entering their bodies from two and sometimes three different directions. The swelling battle line of Gen. W. T. Wofford was pouring out of the woods on the western edge of the Wheatfield, sweeping everything in its path.

Sweitzer's center and left barely had time to escape, but the men of the 4th Michigan were under peril of total envelopment. Regimental formation was sacrificed until a position of safety could be reached, and the Michigan unit was thoroughly disorganized. The color guard was falling one by one as the regiment retraced its steps across the field, and at last the sole color-bearer fell, grasping the staff in his agony. Col. Harrison Jeffords, the commander of the dwindling regiment, saw the man fall and reacted immediately on seeing a Confederate seize the flag from the hand of the suffering color-bearer. Raising his drawn sword, the hatless Jeffords rushed after the Southerner, followed by several other officers and men of the regiment. Jeffords was the first to reach those of the enemy around their newly captured prize, and he cut down the man bearing off the colors with his sword, only to be attacked by several vengeful comrades of the victim. A bayonet thrust through the chest of Colonel Jeffords brought him to his knees, and it was with the utmost difficulty that soldiers of his command were able to carry him off the field and prevent him from falling into enemy hands.

KATHY G. HARRISON

ARTIST COMMENTS

There are several skies in this painting, although the viewer can see only the surface one. For some reason, I was unsatisfied with my earlier attempts and painted over them. Each time, the tree edges needed to be redone to make them crisp against the sky.

The scene with Colonel Jeffords was posed and reposed many different ways until I found one that seemed satisfactory. The flag we were using for the 4th Michigan was torn during the re-created struggle.

DON'T GIVE AN INCH

"Don't Give an Inch."

For many regiments that fought in the Civil War, there was a single incident—perhaps a command, a change in direction, or a delay in their movement—that became their defining moment. For the four regiments of the 3rd Brigade, 1st Division of the Union V Corps, that moment, as it was for many other regiments both North and South, came on July 2, 1863, at the battle of Gettysburg.

Commanded that day by a promising young officer, Col. Strong Vincent, the brigade consisting of the 20th Maine, 83rd Pennsylvania, 44th New York, and the 16th Michigan was making its way to support the embattled Union III

Corps. Upon reaching the George Weikert House on Cemetery Ridge, Vincent observed a staff officer riding toward him. Riding to meet him, Vincent called out. "Captain, what are your orders?" The captain replied, "Where is General Barnes?" Vincent repeated, "What are your orders? Give me your orders." Pointing to Little Round Top, the captain told him, "General Sykes directs Genl. Barnes to send a brigade of his division to occupy that hill yonder." Vincent said, "I will take the responsibility of taking my Brigade there."

Ordering Col. James Rice of the 44th New York to bring the brigade as quickly as possible, Vincent rode ahead

Reference photo taken for "Don't Give an Inch."

to scout the hill and pick positions for his regiments. Shortly after he had selected a position partway down the southern slope of Little Round Top, the brigade arrived. Vincent immediately placed the 20th Maine on the Union left and the 83rd Pennsylvania to its right, followed by the 44th New York. On the right of the brigade was the undersize 16th Michigan Volunteer Infantry.

Taking what cover they could behind the large boulders that were strewn across the hill, the brigade had but a short time to wait, for soon after arriving at their assigned positions Alabamans and Texans of John B. Hood's Confederate division came pouring out of the woods. "They at once attacked the whole line," recalled one Pennsylvanian. "In an instant a sheet of smoke and flames burst from our whole line, which made the enemy reel and stagger." Again the Confederates charged, only to be pushed back again. It was apparent that yet a third Confederate charge was in store for Vincent's brigade. Only this time, the focus of the charge would be on the diminutive 16th Michigan.

Seeing the danger to his right flank, Vincent climbed a large rock and yelled, "Don't yield an inch now or all is lost!" Within moments, he was mortally wounded, shot through the groin. It was only by the efforts of Colonel Vincent and the timely arrival of the 140th New York on the right of the 16th that the brigade's right flank was not turned. Vincent was promoted to brigadier general on July 3, 1863, a rank he held until his death four days later.

KEITH KNOKE

ARTIST COMMENTS

I think this is one of my better efforts. The soldiers placed among the rocks really give this painting a different look, and I enjoy doing rocks. I painted some of the closer rocks in a thick-textured white underpaint, which I scratched with mashed toothpicks and damaged bristle brushes to create an irregular look. After drying, I scoured this over with thin layers of color, which filled the crevices and gave a three-dimensional feel. This technique was used heavily in the seventeenth through nineteenth centuries, but it is not employed much by contemporary artists, perhaps because it's too time-consuming.

In more panoramic views such as this one, the predicament for me is to establish what activity was going on in the distance that would coincide exactly with the foreground action. This is an area that many historians rarely agree on.

The Texas Brigade, 1863.

Paul Loane poses for scale on Little Round Top
during a field trip to Gettysburg.

LITTLE ROUND TOP

On the sizzling-hot afternoon of July 2, 1863, a few thousand Southerners from Texas, Arkansas, and Alabama fought tenaciously for control of a key promontory on the left end of the Union line near Gettysburg. The Confederates and the foe they fought there turned the blood-drenched hilltop into one of the most famous military sites in all of American history.

Gen. John B. Hood's renowned Texas Brigade, now commanded by Gen. Jerome B. Robertson, reached the foreslope of the soon-to-be-famous ridge after a long and wearying approach march. The brigade's four regiments, the 1st, 4th, and 5th Texas and the 3rd Arkansas, had moved toward the battlefield throughout the preceding night. As part of the immense column of Gen. James Longstreet's corps, the brigade had endured a torturous march, beset by detours and complications, toward the south end of the battlefield. Once into the tactical zone, Hood, now commanding the division, sought permission to outflank the Round Tops instead of attacking them frontally.

A few days later, a member of the 5th Texas wrote that "Gen. Hood . . . protested, saying he could take the place very easily by flanking around the mountain, but no, Bullhead Longstreet ordered him to go straight forward and forward we went." The Texans' advance "straight forward" propelled them into one of the most famous conflicts of the Civil War, as they scrambled across the rock-strewn slopes of Little Round Top. Hood went down, having been sorely wounded during the approach.

A Texan fighting in the ranks of the 5th reported that their blue-clad foe enjoyed a "strong position behind rocks upon the top of a hill." He noted, "We fought them about 1 hour the lines being not more than 20 or 30 paces apart." Another Texan estimated the range similarly: "They are not more than 25 or 30 steps away. . . . We are suffering terribly. . . . The roar of artillery and the din of small arms was so deafening that we could not hear each other."

146th New York Volunteer Infantry.

An Arkansas soldier admiringly described the fortitude of his comrades of the 5th Texas, who "rushed across the hill without skirmishers in solid mass, every man pushing forward and yelling like Indians." Col. Robert M. Powell, commanding the 5th Texas, fell wounded into enemy hands. He described the close-range combat as "a devil's carnival" that "raged with wild ferocity."

The Texans' bravery cost them dearly. The 5th lost at least 54 men killed or mortally wounded, among a total of 211 casualties.

ROBERT K. KRICK

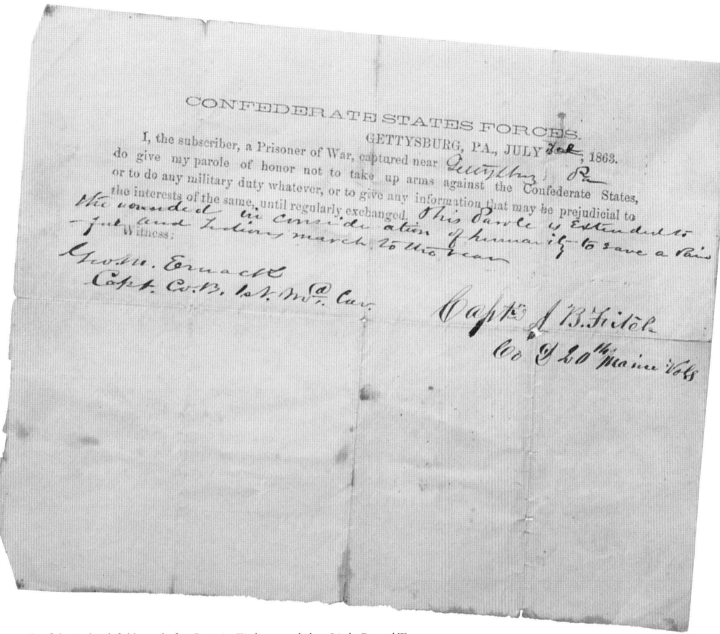

Confederate battlefield parole for Captain Fitch, wounded at Little Round Top. TROIANI COLLECTION

ARTIST COMMENTS

This painting was an effort to portray the advance of the Texans' in a way that had not been illustrated previously. The viewpoint of the Union defenders gives a nice overlook of the Devil's Den area and some of the sweep of the fighting still going on in the valley. Having the Texas brigade headed directly at the viewer is also an equally intimidating vision.

All of the rocks in the painting are the exact ones on the hillside, which still can be found there today. After having pictures taken of the site by Ed Christopher, I posed the models in a rocky section of my backyard, guiding their poses to match the original rocks. Great care was required to paint the bullet strikes on the stones, which would have been quite numerous.

LIONS OF THE ROUNDTOP

"I place you here! This is the left of the Union line. You under-stand. You are to hold this ground at all costs!" For Col. Joshua Lawrence Chamberlain of the 20th Maine Volunteer Infantry, these orders from his brigade commander, Col. Strong Vincent, were as clear as they were ominous. Numbering but 358 men, the 20th Maine took its place on the southwestern slopes of Little Round Top. To their left front lay the northern slopes of Big Round Top, to their right front the large boulders of Devil's Den and the Plum Run Valley. The regiment was in position no more than fifteen minutes when the initial Confederate assaults by portions of Brig. Gen. Evander Law's and Brig. Gen. Jerome Robertson's brigades struck the center of Vincent's line. But these regiments would not be the 20th Maine's primary antagonist; their foe was then approaching from another quarter.

By the late afternoon of July 2, the soldiers of Col. William Oates's 15th Alabama and Col. James W. Jackson's diminutive 47th Alabama were exhausted and thirsty. Having already engaged in a pitched fight with Maj. Homer Stoughton's detachment of Berdan Sharpshooters and climbed and cleared the crest of Big Round Top, the Alabamians were far from fresh, but their work for the day was far from done. Urged onward, the Alabamians began to descend the northern slope of Big Round Top toward the sounds of the engagement on Little Round Top and toward the waiting guns of the 20th Maine.

The 47th Alabama stuck first, charging up the southwestern slope of Little Round Top. "The 47th Alabama," recalled a lieutenant in the 20th Maine, "struck our regiment squarely in front and opened a murderous fire." Shortly after reaching the slopes of the embattled hill, Lt. Col. Michael Bulger, then commanding the regiment, fell wounded, cutting short any momentum the regiment may have had. The 20th Maine hotly engaged with the 47th Alabama, but the 15th Alabama was now arriving on the field, and its intention of gaining the 20th Maine's left flank did not go unob-

Field trip to Little Round Top.

5th New Jersey Infantry.

served. Recalling the event years later, Chamberlain said, "I fortunately observed a body of the enemy moving towards our extreme left . . . which gave me notice of their intention to gain our flank, and gave me time to refuse the left of my line." Thus while the 15th Alabama filed to the right, the 20th Maine made efforts to extend its line to meet this new threat.

On reaching a point to the left and rear of the 20th Maine's original position, wasting little time, Colonel Oates, ordered an advance against the ever-thinning line of Union

defenders. Stepping off in fine order, the Alabamians covered half the distance to the Union line, when they received a well-directed fire. The volley "was so destructive," recalled Oates, "that my line wavered like a man trying to walk against a strong wind." Yet the Alabamians continued to press up the hill, with the Maine men just as stubbornly fighting to hold it.

The fight had become one of attrition. The ebb and flow of this fierce contest began to take their toll on both sides. For Oates, it became apparent that he had insufficient manpower to take the hill, let alone hold it should he do so. Taking this

Model posing with 20th Maine flag for "Lions of the Roundtop."

Identification disc of Sergeant Esterbrooks of the 20th Maine, worn at Gettysburg. TROIANI COLLECTION

into account, along with the realization that no support was forthcoming, Oates ordered the 15th Alabama to withdraw.

At about the same time that Oates was evaluating his options, Colonel Chamberlain concluded he had but one. The 15th Alabama was coming dangerously close to cutting the 20th Maine off from the rest of Vincent's brigade, and the regiment's ammunition supply was rapidly dwindling with little hope of being resupplied. "Desperate as the chances were," recalled Chamberlain, "there was nothing for it, but to take the offensive." Stepping to the colors, Chamberlain ordered,

"Bayonet! . . . Forward!" As it charged downslope, the 20th Maine caught the 15th Alabama in the initial phase of withdrawal, completely shattering any organization the Alabamians may have had.

For Colonel Chamberlain and the soldiers of the 20th Maine, the thrill of the charge and the final outcome were measured only in the thoughts of how close the contest had been. But for the Alabamians, it was an inglorious conclusion to a battle that only moments before had held so much promise of success.

KEITH KNOKE

BARKSDALE'S CHARGE

William Barksdale of Mississippi joined a volunteer company in 1846, intending to help win the Mexican War, but his unit never saw combat. As a politician during the turbulent 1850s, Barksdale found plenty of action—a knife fight, a duel, and a famous fistfight on the floor of the U.S. House of Representatives.

As a colonel and then a brigadier general commanding four hard-fighting Mississippi regiments, the 13th, 17th, 18th, and 21st, Barksdale won distinction in the Seven Days around Richmond and at Sharpsburg. Their tenacious defense of the riverfront at Fredericksburg in December 1862 earned lasting glory for Barksdale and his men.

Late on the afternoon of July 2, 1863, Barksdale's Mississippians followed their general across the Emmitsburg Pike, south of Gettysburg, in a screaming charge that drove an enemy force away from the Peach Orchard and the Sherfy farm. The defenders overwhelmed by Barksdale's brigade included the colorfully accoutered Zouaves of the 114th Pennsylvania. One of the men with Barksdale on that fateful day recalled the general's "thin light hair . . . [and] his forward, impetuous bearing. . . . Stamped on his face . . . was determination 'to do or die.'" Astride a large bay horse and "dressed in a new bright gray uniform," William Barksdale galloped forward in the midst of his troops. A divisional staff officer who watched the general lead the attack, "his face . . . radiant with joy," could follow Barksdale's progress, as his hat was off and his long, white hair stood out like a beacon. When the Mississippians collided with the enemy, the aide noted, "the slaughter of the red-breeched zouaves . . . was terrible."

Across the Emmitsburg Pike, Barksdale's men overcame resistance by two more Pennsylvania regiments and some New Yorkers. The general sought to sustain the brigade's hard-won momentum. "Brave Mississippians, one more charge and the day is ours!" he yelled above the cacophony of battle. The Mississippians responded, but one more charge proved not to be enough. They followed their battle flags forward toward the Trostle farm, with its memorably photographed barn, and then even farther east across the Plum Run bottom. There, Barksdale's luck ran out. A bullet hit his leg, a shell mangled his foot, and a canister round smashed through his chest into a lung. "I am killed," the general muttered to an aide as his consciousness dwindled. "Tell my wife and children that I died fighting at my post."

"He has left us his noble example," Gen. Robert E. Lee wrote to the general's grieving widow. The charge past the Peach Orchard by William Barksdale and his Mississippians stands as one of the most magnificent episodes in the annals of the Army of Northern Virginia.

ROBERT K. KRICK

WALTER WALPIN

PRIVATE COLLECTION

114th Pennsylvania Volunteers, Collis Zouaves.

ARTIST COMMENTS

The most fascinating area of this painting to reconstruct was the Sherfy farmyard in the background. The house is somewhat different today than it was in 1863. An ink sketch done not long after the battle by Benjamin J. Lossing shows no front porch, and the extension on the back was only a single story. The brick house was painted over in a solid red color, a popular trend at the time.

Master clothing maker Charles Childs, who copied originals in my collection, could make only two Collis Zouave replica uniforms for this project. Accordingly, the models could be posed only in pairs, not in larger groupings, and the process of dressing and undressing all those who stood in as Zouaves was long and tedious. Contrary to some modern renderings, the trousers of the 114th were not the full, baggy, scarlet Zouave breeches, but were more like regular straight-legged army trousers made of heavyweight imported French Army brick red material.

Collage of snapshots of the Sherfy farm with a period barn added where the current barn now stands.

Sherfy House as it is today.

Models pose as Collis Zouaves for background of "Barksdale's Charge."

"RETREAT BY RECOIL"

The entire left flank of the Army of the Potomac was ablaze with fighting late on the afternoon of July 2, 1863. Some of the most desperate, hotly contested action involved Capt. John Bigelow's 9th Massachusetts Battery. Early in the action, the unit blasted away at Confederates from its position along the Wheatfield Road, east of the Peach Orchard. As the Southern soldiers intensified their assault, the Union artillery on that part of the battlefield was in dire straits.

Brig. Gen. William Barksdale's brigade of Mississippi regiments smashed into the Union defenses in and around the Peach Orchard. Lt. Col. Freeman McGilvery ordered the Federal gunners to withdraw their cannons before they were overrun. Captain Bigelow's battery was the last to leave the Wheatfield Road, finally heeding McGilvery's order to "limber up and get out." But that command was easier said than done.

Bigelow's concern was that the charging Confederates of the 21st Mississippi would engulf his six Napoleons if his men stopped firing. Desperate for the safety of his battery, he gave orders to retreat by recoil. This difficult maneuver was executed by attaching the ropes from the guns to the limbers and having the horses pull them out. That allowed the guns to be fired during the retreat. The recoil from the firing hurtled the Napoleons backward, assisting in their withdrawal. The battery covered several hundred yards in this fashion, heading toward the Trostle farmyard.

The guns reached a wall at the edge of the lane in front of the Trostle buildings. Bigelow hoped to get his pieces out through a gate in the wall, but it was not to be. McGilvery approached him and ordered Bigelow "to hold his position as long as possible at all hazards." The artillery commander needed to establish a defensive line east of the Trostle farm, and the 9th Massachusetts Battery was going to be the sacrificial lamb to buy time to do so.

Paul Loane during background shooting for "Retreat by Recoil."

Bigelow reacted quickly. He positioned his guns near the fence corner opposite the Trostle farmhouse, arranging the three sections of the battery in a semicircle and having the men pile up the ammunition alongside each gun. Soon the Mississippians streamed over the high ground in front of the Bay Staters, and Bigelow ordered his gunners to fire as rapidly as possible. The guns blazed away for the next several minutes. In the heat of the action, Captain Bigelow saw McGilvery's line of guns forming up 300 yards to his rear. He ordered his sections to try to get away, but that proved nearly impossible, with the stone fence impeding their retreat

As the battery pulled out, three of the guns were captured. Bigelow was wounded and remarkably removed from the field by Bugler Charles Reed, who received a Medal of Honor for his brave actions that afternoon. Bigelow's report attested to the deadly work performed by the 9th Massachusetts Battery that day: It "had fired three tons of ammunition, including 92 rounds of canister, at the enemy."

JAY JORGENSEN

ARTIST COMMENTS

The precise location where this incident occurred has hardly changed from July 1863, a historical artist's dream. Only a few trees needed to be added in their original period locations. I relied heavily on the delightfully factual sketches of Charles Reed, the battery bugler, shown in the painting on the gray horse, for further details.

I initially posed the gunner holding the lanyard in a blue uniform jacket, but after painting him in, I felt that the composition needed more of a central focus. So I reposed him wearing a red flannel shirt, the kind actually favored by Federal artillerymen. The splash of scarlet, which was a complementary color to all the green foliage, did the trick.

U.S. Army Surgeon.

FIRST MINNESOTA

In June 1861, the 1st Minnesota Volunteer Infantry left its home state with more than 1,000 men. By the beginning of July 1863, after two years of hard campaigning, it could muster but 400. But what the regiment lacked in numbers, it more than made up in experience. Already well respected for its feats on the battlefields of First Bull Run, Savage Station, and Antietam, the regiment secured a place in history with its actions at the battle of Gettysburg.

Having spent the night of July 1 in the fields southeast of Little Round Top, the men of 1st Minnesota were aroused early the morning and marched, along with the rest of the Union II Corps, the short distance to the center of the Union line on Cemetery Hill. Here the regiment spent the morning and early afternoon under Confederate artillery fire. Recalling the event years later, a private in Company A wrote, "It is quite a peculiar feeling for a man to stand there on level ground for 3 or 4 hours and be shot at all the time and not being able to defend yourself."

By 4 P.M., Confederate general James Longstreet's aggressive attack on the Union left was well under way, and the overstretched and hard-pressed Union III and V Corps' need for reinforcements was clear. This need was met in part by the men of Brig. Gen. John C. Caldwell's 1st Division of the II Corps, then holding large portion of the Union center. The gap in the Union line caused by the departure of Caldwell's division would be filled, at least for the moment, by a single regiment, the 1st Minnesota. Marching forward and to the left, the regiment formed near the crest of Cemetery Ridge and to the left of Capt. Evan Thomas's Battery C of the 4th U.S. Artillery.

To the regiment's left front, the Union III Corps was desperately trying to hold its line in and around the Peach Orchard. Recalling this struggle, one Minnesotan wrote: "Crashing, crushing, stunning discharges of artillery made the earth vibrate beneath us. Rolling, tearing, crackling volley of musketry, Union cheers and Confederate yells, mingling with other noises of the strife. . . . It was with feelings of anxiety, beyond words to express that we watched the awful scene before us, listened to the tumultuous sounds, and wondered how it would end." One Union company had been lost to provost guard duty and another to picket duty. The remaining eight companies, numbering about 290 officers and men, did not have long to wait before they too were thrown into the melee. Through the smoke and haze, and beyond the now retreating III Corps, the men of the 1st Regiment caught their first glimpse of the long, gray line of Brig. Gen. Cadmus Wilcox's Alabama Brigade.

Reining his horse in behind the eight undersized companies of the 1st Minnesota, Union major general Winfield Scott Hancock exclaimed, "My God, are these all the men we have here?" Knowing he had to delay the advance of the Confederate line until reinforcements could arrive, he asked, "What regiment is this?" "First Minnesota," replied Col. William Colvill. "Charge those lines!" commanded Hancock. "Every man realized in an instant what that order meant," recalled one Minnesotan, "death or wounds to us all."

The 1st Minnesota made the charge, providing the time that Hancock so desperately sought. The cost, by any measure, was extreme. One Minnesotan penned what must have been an all to common thought after the charge: "But good God! Where was the 1st Minnesota? Our flag was carried back to the battery and seventy men . . . are all that formed around it; the other two hundred, alas, lay bleeding under it."

KEITH KNOKE

ARTIST COMMENTS

The charge of this unit at the critical moment has been painted quite a few times in the past, including even once by me. As I was kicking around ideas, it came to me that the suspense before going into battle was rarely the subject of the artist's brush. The anticipation of knowing one is about to face death has to be the most dreaded moment of all.

Here the brave 1st Minnesotans are staring at the Union line crumbling before them. Following directly behind is an overwhelming force of Confederates, flush with victory. These men know that the Southerners cannot be stopped and their lives will be sacrificed to buy time. My aspiration was to show the range of emotions on the soldiers' faces, a mix of fear, doubt, and determination.

Band of Brothers

The lone Maryland infantry unit in Robert E. Lee's army fought a desperate battle on the lower slopes of Culp's Hill on July 2–3, 1863. The costly struggle became one of the most renowned episodes involving Maryland Confederates during the war.

Although they were isolated from their families, who lived out of reach behind enemy lines, and immune to Southern conscription laws, Marylanders carved out a sturdy record in the Army of Northern Virginia through the four years of war. Gray-clad Maryland soldiers had fought with distinction under Gen. Stonewall Jackson in the famed 1862 campaign in the Shenandoah Valley and followed him to the outskirts of Richmond to help prevent the pending siege of the capital city. They participated in the liberation of Winchester in June 1863, then welcomed the opportunity to cross the Potomac River to their native soil en route to a date with destiny near Gettysburg, Pennsylvania.

The 1st Maryland Battalion had clung to a precarious lodgment on Culp's Hill through the night of July 2. The next morning, exhausted, hungry, and diminished by casualties, the survivors received orders to attack a powerful enemy force. "It was an impossible task," a Maryland soldier wrote. "Yet there was no flinching . . . no murmuring at the sacrifice they were called on to make. . . . Their splendid heroism was a futile sacrifice. The men fell like leaves before the winter blast."

As they stepped into the open, the Marylanders came under scalding fire from an enemy sheltered in woods beyond the field, where a strong force from the Federal XII Corps occupied an impervious position. By ironic coincidence, a few of the Union troops were Marylanders too. The Southerners bravely dashed forward, but in vain and at daunting cost. "On they pressed to within about twenty or thirty paces of the works—a small but gallant band of heroes daring to attempt what could not be done by flesh and blood."

Some 500 Maryland men and boys went into action at Gettysburg. Nearly half of them fell in the battle. Their commander, the twenty-nine-year-old Lt. Col. James R. Herbert, suffered wounds in his leg, arm, and abdomen and fell into enemy hands.

Robert K. Krick

1st and 2nd Maryland Infantry, C.S.A.

GREENSBORO HISTORY MUSEUM

ARTIST COMMENTS

Here my object was to show the iron discipline of the Mary-landers as they pushed forward where no other troops would go. The contrast of the upright troops rushing past the others hugging the ground helped create the illusion of speed. I spent a good deal of time with the prone models, trying to get them in realistic attitudes. The figure on the far left-hand corner is important since he helps return the viewer's eye back to the center of interest.

Hampton's Duel

At just under six feet tall, Confederate brigadier general Wade Hampton was an imposing figure. His skill as a horseman as well as his devil-may-care bravado made him well suited for the cavalry, and by the summer of 1863, this cavalier found himself in command of a well-seasoned cavalry brigade.

During the Gettysburg campaign, Hampton's skill as a horseman and physical prowess would be put the test. On the afternoon of July 3, 1863, Hampton, his head no doubt still aching from a bloody saber wound he had received the day before, was leading his brigade in Confederate major general Jeb Stuart's objective of protecting the Confederate left flank, located south and east of Gettysburg. But when they approached the John Rummel farm, any hope that Stuart may have had of taking the initiative and sidestepping the Union right flank and attacking the Union rear was dashed. At the intersection of the Hanover and Lower Dutch Roads, squarely between Stuart and the Union rear, were the troopers of Union brigadier general David M. Gregg's Cavalry Division. In between the two lay the open, rolling fields of the Rummel farm, and it was here that decisive cavalry action of the Gettysburg campaign was fought.

The initial engagement between Stuart and Gregg in and around the Rummel farm buildings, although pitched at times, was indecisive. Recognizing the need for decisive action, and seeing an opportunity to separate the Union forces and possibly destroying them in detail, Stuart ordered the brigades of John Chambliss, Fitzhugh Lee, and Wade Hampton to charge. The advance of Confederate horsemen did not fail to impress their Union counterparts. "A grander spectacle than their advance has rarely been beheld," recalled one Pennsylvania trooper. "They marched with well aligned fronts and steady reins. Their polished saber blades dazzled in the sun."

As Stuart's intention became clear, Gregg saw that the decisive action of the day was at hand, at the same time realizing he had few resources left to wage it. He ordered the lone and final Union reserve, the 1st Michigan Volunteer Cavalry, to charge. Drawing his sword, Col. Charles Town, commanding the 1st Michigan, cried: "Draw saber! Remember men be steady, be calm, be firm! Think of Michigan! Forward March!" The two sides met "like falling of timber, so sudden and violent that many of the horses were turned end over end," crushing their riders beneath them.

Not wanting to leave the 1st Michigan to face the onslaught singlehandedly, other Union regiments now began to pitch into the flanks of the charging Confederate column. Capt. James H. Hart's squadron of the 1st New Jersey left the projection of the Low Dutch Road and charged into the unsuspecting Confederate left flank directly toward a Confederate officer of rank, Brig. Gen. Wade Hampton. Riding his favorite mount, Butler, Hampton turned to meet the onrushing New Jersey troopers, bringing one down with his saber and another with his pistol. "While he parried manfully the blows being rained on his devoted head" one Union trooper managed to land a saber blow, reopening his wound from the day before. Soon another blow to the head and wound to the leg left the South Carolinian dazed and bloody.

Coming to their general's aid, a few stalwart Confederate troopers fought desperately to free the embattled South Carolinian. Succeeding in clearing an avenue of escape, Sgt. Nat Price of the 1st North Carolina yelled, "General, general, they are too many for us. For God's sake leap your horse over the fence, I'll die before they have you." Needing no further encouragement, Hampton leaped Butler over the fence, reaching safety. Hampton's wounds proved to be more painful than serious, and by November 1863, he was promoted to major general and commanded a division.

KEITH KNOKE

NATIONAL CIVIL WAR MUSEUM, HARRISBURG, PENNSYLVANIA

ARTIST COMMENTS

Cavalry scenes are the most taxing to re-create, as the artist must manage not only the models, but also the horses, which do not always listen to what they are told. Sometimes I have posed fully mounted troopers with correct tack at a stable for action scenes. With luck, this can sometimes lead to good results, but in this case, it was not possible to have both horses and riders achieve what was needed simultaneously. Accord-ingly, a return to the traditional nineteenth-century artists' way of dealing with this predicament was called for. A carpen-ter made me a heavy wooden saddle stand, fully able to sup-port a rider mounted on a saddle in any position. The horses first were posed, and then the riders in the attitudes required. Through this technique, even those who have never ridden previously, can appear to be superb horsemen on canvas.

THE EMMITSBURG ROAD

At sixty-one years of age, Maj. Gen. Isaac Ridgeway Trimble was among the oldest Confederates present at Gettysburg. He was also one of the last officers to reach the field and assume command responsibilities.

The Virginia native and West Point graduate had been associated with Maryland for several decades and had carved out a successful career in engineering and railroads. In 1861, he joined Confederate service and quickly made a reputation for aggressive leadership. The old fellow hated Yankees and relished fighting them. A cavalryman who encountered the general in 1862 marveled at his brusqueness, describing Trimble as "a small man with a naked sword in his hand" who loudly inquired, "Who the hell is this gentleman?"

A severe wound at Second Manassas interrupted Trimble's career, but he abandoned his long convalescence to follow the Army of Northern Virginia into Pennsylvania in June 1863. At Carlisle, he volunteered as an aide to Gen. Richard Ewell, and at Gettysburg, he assumed command of the mortally wounded Maj. Gen. Dorsey Pender's division. Almost immediately, he led a portion of his temporary command forward in what became known as Pickett's Charge.

The renowned attack on the Federal center on July 3, 1863, actually included far more troops than Pickett's Virginians. Trimble rode forward in the midst of the North Carolinians of his new command, next to the flag of the 7th North Carolina. A member of the 7th described advancing through "a withering fire of shot and shell," with the Carolina soldiers "cheering for the 'Old North State' with such volume of voice as to be heard above the din of battle."

When Trimble's men reached the Emmitsburg Road, a sturdy post-and-rail fence impeded their advance. The wooden fence, built in peacetime for civilian purposes, proved almost as good an obstacle as a military abatis would have been. Some men halted behind it. Others climbed over, pounded by Northern fire as they did so, prompting Trimble to boast to an aide, "I believe those fine fellows are going into the enemy's lines." Almost all of the few who accomplished that feat died in the attempt. "Had there been no fence in the way," a Tarheel wrote, more wistfully than logically, they "would have driven the Federals from their line."

Trimble's brief return to command ended that afternoon when a disabling wound cost him a leg. He became a Northern prisoner at Gettysburg and never returned to the army.

ROBERT K. KRICK

Post-and-board fence in Gettysburg at the site of Trimble's attack.

ARTIST COMMENTS

In order to accurately portray soldiers clambering over a post-and-board fence, I took my models to a local stable that had a similar type fencing. Valiantly in the summer heat, they repeatedly catapulted themselves over the obstacle until I felt I had enough material. Then I selected the best and most natural-looking poses from the hundreds of shots taken. Credible attitudes were achieved when the models actually clambered over the rails. The soldiers falling backward were the most dangerous to position, and it took several others to hold them up.

Give Them Cold Steel, Boys

Confederate general Lewis A. Armistead created one of the most familiar and stirring images in all of American military history when he led his Virginia brigade to the forefront of the immortal charge by Pickett's division at Gettysburg on July 3, 1863. Shouting to his men as he strode to certain death with his hat carried on the tip of his sword, Armistead passed into American legend that hot afternoon. He remains perhaps the best known of the brigade commanders in the storied Army of Northern Virginia because of that final vivid episode of his life.

Armistead's route to Gettysburg had carried him across North America as an Old Army officer. "I have been a soldier all my life," he wrote in 1861, and he gave up what little he had managed to accrue of means when he left the U.S. Army.

The regiments of Armistead's brigade had seen combat near Richmond in 1862, but every man looking across the fields near Gettysburg could tell that July 3 would be deadly beyond imagining. While instructing his chief surgeon that he would "have much to do," Armistead revealed his forebodings: "Doctor, all hell is going to turn loose here within fifteen minutes. . . . The slaughter will be terrible."

When the moment to begin the charge arrived, Lewis Armistead strode in front of his men and gave the order that would be fatal to so many of them. "He was an old army officer," a lieutenant wrote, "and was possessed of a very loud voice."

Casualties dropped steadily out of ranks as the Virginians came under artillery fire, but they fell in horrible windrows once in musketry range. As the attackers approached the low rock fence where Federal soldiers waited, Armistead turned to the commander of the 53rd Virginia Infantry and said, "Colonel, double quick." The colonel shouted for a renewed advance but almost at once fell severely wounded. At the wall, Armistead called out to his men: "Come on, boys, give them the cold steel! Who will follow me?"

The general's hat eventually slid down the cold steel shaft of his sword, and he carried it forward that way, the sun glinting off his bare and balding head. Next to the Federal guns, Armistead went down, mortally wounded in a leg and arm, leaving a handful of survivors to ebb away from the high-water mark and begin a long, painful retreat back to Virginia.

ROBERT K. KRICK

ARTIST COMMENTS

This panorama showing masses of men presented me with significant problems in laying out the composition. I also needed to be careful to impart a sense of place so that some background areas would be discernible and the entire work would not be just a heap of jumbled humanity. I silhouetted General Armistead against the sky to distinguish him as the center of interest and placed him at the right of the painting to suggest forward motion. I posed as the model for the soldier on the lower left with his posterior to the viewer, as I could not demonstrate to the models exactly what was needed. In those days I was thin enough, but no longer.

Don working on "Give Them Cold Steel, Boys" in 1987. RON TUNISON

With model Jeff Marks, posing for "Give Them Cold Steel, Boys."

72nd Pennsylvania Volunteers, Baxter's Zouaves.

PRIVATE COLLECTION

2nd Corps badge worn by a Baxter Zouave.

TROIANI COLLECTION

TOWARD THE ANGLE

Forty-five-year-old Gen. Richard Brooke Garnett rode across the open farm fields south of Gettysburg on July 3, 1863, at the head of a brigade of five Virginia regiments. He had been a professional soldier for nearly three decades and had served across the full breadth of the continent, but nothing could have prepared him for the maelstrom of fire that would kill him near the Emmitsburg Pike on this cataclysmic afternoon.

Dick Garnett was one of twins born in 1817 in Essex County, Virginia. After graduating twenty-ninth out of fifty-two from West Point in 1841, Garnett began his career as a second lieutenant in the 6th U.S. Infantry. During twenty years in the army, he never left that unit except on temporary assignments. He served on the fringes of the Mexican War; on the Great Plains, where he left behind a half-Sioux son and barely escaped a famous massacre; and in the "Mormon War." Eventually he led troops across the Sierra Nevada to California. By 1861, Garnett had risen only to the rank of captain—a typical progression in the tiny prewar army.

In March 1862, Dick Garnett earned the enmity of the inflexible Stonewall Jackson when he pulled his brigade out of line at the battle of Kernstown to avoid being overwhelmed. Robert E. Lee assigned the unhappy brigadier to George E. Pickett's former brigade in the I Corps, away from the control of the unforgiving Jackson. By July 1863, Garnett had commanded the brigade for ten months. One of his subordinates

described the brigadier with mixed reviews: "Not a man of much mental force [but] one of the noblest and bravest men I ever knew."

En route to Gettysburg, a staff officer's "fiery steed" kicked Garnett's ankle and badly crippled him. On June 25,

the general remained worried about how soon he would be able to ride again. Eight days later, Garnett rode a bay mare toward the enemy line on Cemetery Ridge. When Northern fire killed the mare, he mounted a bay gelding, an animal of "fractious spirit," and resumed the advance. Garnett's lifelong

comrade in arms, Gen. Lewis A. Armistead, advanced on foot nearby. Near the high-water mark of this most famous charge in American history, both Garnett and Armistead, comrades for so many long years, met with fatal bullets within a few moments and yards of each other.

ROBERT K. KRICK

"ROCK OF ERIN"

On July 3, 1863, the center of the Union line was manned by the II Corps. Brig. Gen. Alexander Webb's Philadelphia Brigade was positioned at a copse of trees. The 69th Pennsylvania was part of that brigade, and many of the soldiers in the regiment were of Irish descent. Sensing renewed hostilities later in the day, the members of the 69th Pennsylvania spent much of that morning collecting and stockpiling abandoned weapons nearby. They loaded the rifles with buckshot removed from the ball and buckshot cartridges they had.

When a great artillery barrage opened up early in the afternoon, the men hunkered down and weathered the rain of shot and shell. General officers including Alexander Hays and John Gibbon rode along the line trying to reassure the men. Finally the cannonading stopped and 12,500 Confederates began the immortal Pickett's Charge, coming right for the copse of trees and the Philadelphia Brigade.

Col. Dennis O'Kane of the 69th Pennsylvania addressed his men. He reminded them that they were fighting for hearth and home on their native soil. He challenged the men to stay at their post and see to it that those around them did the same. O'Kane's other piece of advice was for the men to hold their fire against the Confederates until they "could distinguish the whites of their eyes."

Soon enough the Southern horde crossed the Emmitsburg Road, and the Union line erupted with gunfire. The extra loaded weapons enabled the soldiers in the 69th Pennsylvania to put up a galling, rapid fire. Nonetheless, the enemy closed in on them, charging to the wall in front of the copse of trees, where the fighting was hand-to-hand. Gen. Lewis Armistead pierced the Union line and led 200 to 300 soldiers into the gap on the right of the 69th Pennsylvania.

The three right companies of the 69th Pennsylvania, I, A, and F, tried to re-fuse their line to meet that threat. Only Companies I and A were able to carry out that maneuver, as Capt. George Thompson of Company F was killed giving the order. Fortunately for the men of Erin, help was on the way, and the Confederates were pushed back. The losses in the regiment were severe, but the men could hold their heads high knowing they had served their adopted country well by fighting so tenaciously in the fury that was Pickett's Charge.

JAY JORGENSEN

ARTIST COMMENTS

No green flags of the 69th Pennsylvania Volunteers are known to remain. Although descriptions are somewhat detailed, they really could not provide the basis for a reconstruction that I felt would be accurate enough. Therefore, I chose to show the colors draped. Should the day come that an actual flag surfaces in some forgotten Philadelphia attic, I hope I was not far off in my limited reconstruction.

On-site picture of the clump of trees area for "Rock of Erin."

HIGH WATER MARK

Gen. Lewis Addison Armistead (pronounced with two syllables, as Arm-sted or Um-sted) came from a family rich in military tradition. His uncle George Armistead had commanded Fort McHenry in Baltimore Harbor in 1814 during the defense that inspired Francis Scott Key to write "The Star Spangled Banner." Lewis's father, Walker Keith Armistead, became a general officer in the U.S. Army when Lewis was eleven. Most other male Armisteads had been soldiers.

After an uneven career at West Point, Lewis Armistead led troops all across the American frontier. He lost his wife to disease in Kansas. On August 5, 1859, the detachment he commanded near the Arizona-California border won a bitter engagement with about 200 Mojaves. The hostiles "stood our fire very well," Major Armistead reported, "coming up to within twenty and thirty paces."

In his pitched battle with Indians, Armistead had more experience commanding in prewar combat than did most other officers destined to fight as Civil War generals. But that experience, as well as leading his brigade at Seven Pines and Malvern Hill, bore little resemblance to the inferno that faced Armistead at the climax of Pickett's Charge at Gettysburg on July 3, 1863.

Armistead's brigade of Virginia regiments—the 9th, 14th, 38th, 53rd, and 57th—began its march toward destiny in crisp alignment. "Look at my line," the general boasted to a comrade; "it never looked better on dress parade." Shells tore gaps in the regiments as they crossed the fields toward distant Cemetery Ridge. When the Virginians closed with their foe, sheets of musketry shredded the Southern ranks. The pretty line dissolved into a disorganized but still determined band that pressed bravely onward.

Ed Vebell and Paul Loane during background photography at Gettysburg in the late 1980s.

Confederate infantry corporal.

With his hat perched on the tip of his sword, Lewis Armistead led his survivors over a low stone fence and into a densely defended Federal stronghold. The Northern troops they faced belonged to the II Corps, commanded by Armistead's dear friend from the Old Army, Gen. Winfield Scott Hancock. The 69th and 71st Pennsylvania fired into the Virginians, and Lt. Alonzo H. Cushing's battery hurled canister at the attackers. One of the Yankees saw Armistead "yelling something to his men," and then the general "caught hold of the left wheel of the [cannon] and fell right there."

Wounds in Armistead's leg and arm proved mortal. A few weeks later, a Pennsylvanian dug up the Virginian's corpse and embalmed it, because "he thought Armistead['s] friends would pay a good price for his body."

ROBERT K. KRICK

ARTIST COMMENTS

Backlighting is always a challenge, but when properly executed, the results can be show-stopping. I like to try to achieve effects such as this one, with the light passing through the thin wool bunting material of the Confederate flags. To obtain this effect, the flag was waved in front of the late-afternoon sun, whose rays filtered through it and rimmed the edges with a wonderful glow.

Quantrill's Guerrillas.

EAGLE OF EIGHTH

Captured as a nestling eaglet by a Chippewa Indian in early 1861, Old Abe had been traded to a local farmer as a family pet. He was offered to and purchased by Capt. John E. Perkins, then forming the Eau Claire Badgers in Chippewa County, Wisconsin. Assigned to the 8th Regiment Wisconsin Volunteer Infantry as its Company C, the Eau Claire Badgers became the color company of the regiment. At Camp Randall in Madison, Wisconsin's quartermaster general provided Old Abe with a special wooden perch painted with the red, white, and blue shield of the U.S. coat of arms. At the battle of Corinth, on October 3, 1862, an enemy bullet cut the cord that tethered Old Abe to his perch, permitting him to fly free along the line of his embattled regiment, losing several feathers to enemy fire in the process.

On May 22, 1863, Old Abe and the 8th Wisconsin found themselves in the trenches opposite Stockade Redan at the juncture of Vicksburg's northern and eastern defenses. Gen. Joseph A. Mower's brigade, which included the 8th Wisconsin, was selected to carry out a forlorn attack. An officer of the 8th remembered the effect of the artillery as he double-quicked down the road: "We actually stepped on the dead and wounded in the sunken road, so thickly were they lying." Company C, with Old Abe and the colors of the 8th, was in the middle of the column. Just as it exited the declivity, a charge of enemy canister tore into its ranks. At the rear of the company, Old Abe lunged from his perch, screeching, just as his bearer tripped and fell against a stump, temporarily stunning bearer and bird. Eventually both reached the safety of the ravine to the right, where Company C and some survivors from the leading companies were attempting to re-form.

Old Abe, the survivors of Company C, and other companies took shelter in the ravine under intense fire, which riddled the 8th's flags. Hostilities finally ceased with nightfall, and the 8th and her sister regiments retreated to their trenches with their dead and wounded.

In the spring of 1864, Old Abe and the 8th Wisconsin participated in the Red River campaign, including the battles of Pleasant Hill, Cloutiersville, Mansura, and Lake Chicot in Arkansas. In September, Old Abe joined the nonveterans of the 8th in returning again to Wisconsin. There he was turned over to the state and cared for in the capital, though he participated in several Sanitary Commission fund-raising fairs in 1865 and eventually was sent as a live exhibit to the 1876 Centennial Exposition in Philadelphia. A smoky fire in the capital in February 1881 ended the famous bird's career.

HOWARD M. MADAUS

ARTIST COMMENTS

Finding a live bald eagle to pose for Old Abe presented a real problem. I finally heard that the nearby Bridgeport Zoo had a few. It was a scorching day, and the birds were lethargic. The prospect of have a perturbed eagle as a model was fading until the keeper showed up with some tidbits for them. Straightaway they sprung to life, squawking and flapping their wings, while my camera fired away. I got exactly what I required. At the time of the battle, Old Abe was immature and had not yet developed the classic bald eagle's white head and tail feathers.

The eagle at the Bridgeport Zoo.

U. S. Grant

This painting was commissioned for the cover of Newt Gingrich's alternative history of the Civil War, *Grant Comes East*. Maj. Gen. Ulysses S. Grant was to be shown as he appeared in 1863. As I examined photos of the general with his steeds, it became immediately evident that Grant, not a tall man, usually rode very large horses indeed. Also, he seemed to favor a full dress general's shabraque and fairly elegant trappings, in stark contrast to his often austere, and sometimes slovenly, personal dress. Many great generals of history, such as Napoleon, Lee, and Wellington, frequently wore modest attire.

1st South Carolina Volunteer Infantry, U.S. Colored Troops.

WILLIAM GLADSTONE

CLEBURNE AT CHICKAMAUGA

Maj. Gen. Patrick R. Cleburne had the reputation of being a soldier's general, a commander who led from the front. On the afternoon of September 20, 1863, in the forests of Chickamauga, he led his fabled division into an assault on the Federal breastworks that ringed the Kelly farm.

Cleburne had spent most of the afternoon preparing his men to go into action again after their bloody repulse that morning, which had seen the death of one of his brigade commanders, Gen. James Deshler. As Confederate attacks were being beaten back along the slopes of Snodgrass Hill a mile to the west, Cleburne received orders to renew the battle on the Confederate right. At 3:30 P.M., he led his men forward toward the Federal barricades. One soldier in the 2nd Tennessee later described it:

> A terrible burst of artillery and musketry greeted our appearance. The hissing of the missiles was more noticeable than the explosions of the guns, and sounded like the clashings of a multitude of sword blades in the air overhead. Colonel Robison gave the order to charge . . . unfortunately, parts of the line began to fire, which occasioned a halt, and soon the firing became general. No further attempt was made to go forward, as all commands were drowned in the noise of conflict, and the men seemed constrained by circumstances to endure the pelting of the terrible tempest as best they could.

Through all of this, Cleburne was seen along the lines encouraging his men on. At one point, as the ammunition of Lucius Polk's brigade gave out, Cleburne along with his staff had ammunition run to the front, and he began to walk the line, passing packs of rounds to the men. With the renewed ammunition the Confederates were able to push forward and overrun the Federal breastworks that had tormented them all day. In the aftermath of the battle, the extent of Cleburne's exposure could be seen in his after-action report, where he commented on the gallantry of his staff and listed four of the ten named as wounded in action.

LEE WHITE

ARTIST COMMENTS

In my quest to paint all the major battles of the Civil War, one crucial engagement of the West, Chickamauga, remained conspicuously absent. When reading accounts of the battle, I could not find a topic that made a satisfactory subject for a painting. Thoughts of Nathan Bedford Forrest or the Texas Brigade swirled through my head, but though noted battle-field historian Lee White supplied me with much detailed information on both of these topics, I just could not develop an idea that I was satisfied with. I mentioned to Lee an account I had heard about that he was unfamiliar with, which described Gen. Patrick Cleburne and his staff handing out ammunition to his men during the fighting. But I couldn't find it in my notes or recall who had told me about it. About the time I thought I had lost my mind, Lee had a discussion with my good friend Bob Parker, a western theater expert, who mentioned the incident to him. It turned out that it was Bob who had told me about it several years earlier. Bob sent me the paper references, and the project finally got under way.

ANATOMY OF A PAINTING

This is the idea sketch, which turned out to be only a rough guideline compared with the finished work.

Thumbnail idea sketches that I brought to the model shoot as a guide to posing the models.

After posing the models, the initial sketch on the primed board was commenced. I prefer to work with a fairly detailed pencil drawing of the main figures. I often draw in the background figures and landscape with a brush as the scene develops. In a sketch such as this, the tree trunks are usually just drawn in as vertical lines for placements. It is usually best to do the sky first and then paint leaves over that, always taking care to distribute the trees at uneven distances from each other to create a naturally random appearance.

Model posing for soldier removing lid from ammunition box.

My niece, Jessica, models the Hardee flag for me.

The color-bearer's face is beginning to be roughed in.

4th Tennessee Cavalry, C.S.A. Black Trooper, 1863.

WILLIAM GLADSTONE

21st Ohio Volunteer Infantry.

PRIVATE COLLECTION

Colonel of the Confederacy.

LEE'S TEXANS

Within a few weeks after assuming command of the Army of Northern Virginia in June 1862, Gen. Robert E. Lee revolutionized the circumstances facing his newborn nation. At the head of his victorious troops, Lee drove his foes away from Richmond and relocated the war to the outskirts of the enemy capital at Washington. During triumphant campaigns at Fredericksburg and Chancellorsville, the commanding general maneuvered his army with skill and poise. Despite disappointing results at Gettysburg in July 1863, the army had remained in hand and responsive.

In the spring of 1864, the tide began to ebb against the Confederacy. Deprived of the services of his matchless executive officer, Stonewall Jackson, and struggling against ever-increasing enemy resources, Lee faced changed circumstances. Four times within one week, he attempted to lead his men into battle personally, counting on his stature to inspire the troops and reverse disastrous situations. The first and most famous of these episodes occurred on May 6.

Two of the three infantry corps of Lee's army had given a good account of themselves in the thickets of the Wilderness on May 5. When Gen. George G. Meade's Army of the Potomac attempted to cross the Rapidan River and head toward Richmond, Lee's men came roaring eastward and crashed into the enemy flank. Fighting raged along two road corridors until darkness fell. If the missing I Corps of Lee's army under James Longstreet did not arrive in time on May 6, the Confederate line surely would collapse.

Early on the sixth, Gen. Winfield Scott Hancock flung the tough Federal veterans of his II Corps down the Orange Plank Road. The attack dissolved Lee's disorganized remnants and pushed the Southern army to the brink of disaster. Barely in time, Longstreet's advance elements hurried into line. North of the road, in the open fields of the Widow Tapp's farm, the situation remained desperate.

As Lee contemplated the mounting chaos, the first reinforcements surged into the open area. "Who are you?" Lee asked them. When they said they were the Texas Brigade, the matchless shock troops who had fought under Gen. John B. Hood through the army's great campaigns, Lee waved his hat and yelled, "Hurrah for Texas!" The Texans, commanded by Gen. John Gregg, formed and headed for the cauldron of fire in front, and Lee quietly rode into the line to advance with them. The men, some with tears in their eyes, yelled, "Go back General, go back, we won't go in until you go back." An enlisted man grasped the reins of Lee's horse, Traveller, and turned its head to the rear. Lee "stops & to our great relief turns back," a soldier wrote.

The Texans carried a few more than 800 men into action and suffered casualties exceeding 500, redeeming their promise to Lee at enormous cost. A staff officer describing the scene in a contemporary letter wondered, "Was there ever a finer scene for a historical painter?"—a century and a quarter before Don Troiani put brush to canvas to accomplish that result.

ROBERT K. KRICK

ARTIST COMMENTS

I considered this to be my first major Civil War painting, and our company made it into a limited-edition print. When I began working on it, I was still living in a high-rise apartment in downtown Stamford, Connecticut, and posed the entire painting in the building's outdoor parking lot. The models dressed in my seventh-floor apartment and then rode the elevator down to the lobby. Noted sculptor and longtime friend Ron Tunison came over to pose for the Texan with the leveled rifle. Surprisingly, all these wildly dressed and heavily armed men running around the parking lot rarely occasioned much comment. It was a bother, though, having to stop and move the models whenever a car backed out of a parking space. I worked this way for a few years, until 1985, when I moved to Southbury, which provided some real acreage to work on.

This was one of the first modern Civil War prints to show a specific event with actual fighting. Gallery owners were concerned that particular subjects might not appeal to a broad audience and that combat would prove unpopular, especially among women. They were wrong. In fact, it wasn't long until collectors wanted event-specific subject matter almost exclusively.

Confederate Standard Bearer

ARTIST COMMENTS

This was the painting that fully launched my career in the field of Civil War art, but I almost didn't paint it at all. Very few straight Civil War prints had been done at this point, and it was an unknown market in the early 1980s. Not being sure of any collector interest, I did it just for the fun of it. But immediately after release, a gallery in Gettysburg sold fifty over one weekend, an incredible number, and there were disputes among potential buyers that nearly came to fisticuffs when the supply ran out. It was an eye-opener, and I was excited to find that people couldn't wait to buy what I liked to do best.

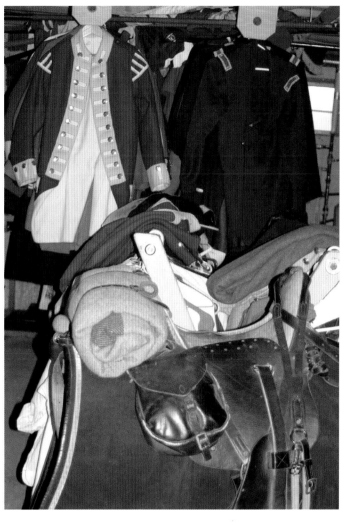

*The artist's uniform
prop department.*

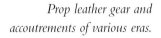

*Prop leather gear and
accoutrements of various eras.*

Bonnie Blue Flag

Stephen Dodson Ramseur graduated from the U.S. Military Academy at West Point just a few months before his native state of North Carolina seceded from the Union. The young soldier forged a strong record at the head of a battery, then a regiment, during the early battles of the Civil War.

When Gen. George B. Anderson died of wounds suffered at Sharpsburg, Ramseur took command of his old brigade, made up of the 2nd, 4th, 14th, and 30th North Carolina.

By mid May 1864, the balding twenty-six-year-old had molded his four-regiment brigade into an eminently reliable military implement. The Carolinians and their leader needed every bit of their experience and élan to cope with the challenge they faced on the foggy, rainy, bloody morning of May 12. Gen. George G. Meade's Army of the Potomac seized the initiative that morning, throwing a dense block of infantry against the nose of a deep salient projecting from the Confederate lines.

Gen. Robert E. Lee had incautiously incorporated the dangerous bulge into his defenses, coveting the high ground it occupied and confident of the strong fortifications defending it. Meade's attackers shattered the center of the salient by 5:30 A.M., leaving Lee's whole army in peril. Confederate defenders staunchly held the shoulders of the salient, even after the nose had been obliterated. The triumphant Northern attackers lost their organization and focus as they plunged southward, and Lee began attempts to restore his lines. By dint of unimaginable bravery and at great loss, Southern troops pushed back toward their original lines.

Fighting raged with particular violence on the western face of the salient. Lee assigned to Ramseur the daunting, deadly task of retaking the works there. West of the McCoull house, midway across the sloping field leading up to their target, the Carolinians paused at a modest intermediate line of works to reorganize their lines "amidst a perfect hail of bullets and shell." Not far to their front swarmed "a living mass of Yankees, in full view."

A Federal round killed Ramseur's horse, then another smashed into the general's right forearm. As Ramseur struggled to maintain control through his pain, under a steady rain and a killing torrent of musketry, one of his men began singing the popular Southern war song "The Bonnie Blue Flag" at the top of his lungs:

> *We are a band of brothers*
> *Native to the soil*
> *Fighting for our liberties*
> *With treasure, blood, and toil.*

Pvt. Tisdale Stepp of Company F, 14th North Carolina Infantry, a twenty-three-year-old farmer from the mountains near Asheville, started the song, and his comrades joined in. When the inspired brigade dashed forward in its final attack, Stepp did not go with the band of brothers. His dramatic moment, singing lustily under fire, had been his last. His colonel reported, with "sore grief, little softened by the lapse of years," that Stepp had been "shot dead by an awkward soldier in our rear rank." General Ramseur survived that desperate May morning but had only four more months to live.

ROBERT K. KRICK

NATIONAL CIVIL WAR MUSEUM, HARRISBURG, PENNSYLVANIA

155th Pennsylvania Volunteers.

ARTIST COMMENTS

Attempting to put on canvas a scene where singing is the theme requires very circumspect posing. If not strongly done, the spectator will not be able to comprehend what is going on. A great many tries were required to establish what I felt was a credible singing pose. I silhouetted Private Stepp against the smoke and mist to bring the viewer's eye directly to him. The late Civil War collector Wendell Lang, a longtime friend, gladly consented to pose for the wounded soldier in the left corner of the painting. Wendell had a great "old veteran" look, chiseled face loaded with character, and was a superb natural model. I hope this will serve as a nice miniportrait of him for posterity.

RANGER MOSBY

MICHAEL FLANAGAN

Born December 6, 1833, in Powhatan County, Virginia, John Singleton Mosby was destined to become one of the South's greatest partisan rangers. A Southern Democrat, he initially was opposed to secession, but when Abraham Lincoln became president and the Civil War began in America, Virginia seceded and Mosby joined the Washington Mounted

Rifles, led by Capt. William "Grumble" Jones. Mosby fought at First Manassas on July 21, 1861, and then became a scout for Confederate cavalry leader Jeb Stuart.

During Union general George B. McClellan's Peninsula Campaign in 1862, the diminutive Mosby played an important part in Stuart's famous ride around the Union army. He later staunchly supported his commander when Stuart was vilified at Gettysburg. Subsequently, he was captured by Yankee cavalry and sent off to the Old Capitol Prison in Washington, where he spent about ten days. Following that incarceration, Mosby was granted permission to organize his group of rangers into the 43rd Virginia Cavalry. Though he raised a total of about 2,000 men during his service, his famous raids never included more than 350 men at a time. In early 1863, during one of Mosby's most famous forays, he captured Union general Edwin H. Stoughton.

The partisan colonel soon won the nom de guerre of the "Gray Ghost" because of his elusive nature and ability to effect lightning strikes without warning. He was never taken out of action permanently, which frustrated the Yankees. Brandishing a pair of pistols, Mosby created his notorious image, which was accentuated by his ostrich-plumed hat, scarlet-lined cloak, and uncanny ability to avoid capture. Frequently operating in a Virginia area known as "Mosby's Confederacy," the celebrated guerrilla traveled the lands around Middleburg, Thoroughfare Gap, Upperville, and Snicker's Gap.

His fame grew as the war continued, and Yankee commander Ulysses S. Grant issued orders that if caught, Mosby should be put to the gallows without trial. After the conflict, however, Mosby returned to a law career, and he and Grant grew close. When Grant's terms as president expired, Mosby supported Rutherford B. Hayes and formally joined the Republican party. President Hayes appointed him the U.S. consul in Hong Kong, which was followed by other positions in politics and government that continued through President Theodore Roosevelt. Mosby died at age eighty-two in 1916, but his fame and legend live on into the present, often making their way into modern television shows, popular art, wineries, taverns, and even board games.

A. M. GAMBONE

3rd New Jersey Cavalry.   PRIVATE COLLECTION

ARTIST COMMENTS

Finding interesting-looking models for Civil War paintings is never easy. Although many are willing, only a small percentage have a nineteenth-century look to them. Because of the constant marching and insufficient diet, most soldiers were extremely lean.

Extra care must be taken, when models are dressed identically to emphasize individuality. Even the shadows cast by the similar headgear can generate a look of sameness in the group. It is essential that each soldier, although wearing the same cap as his neighbors, dons it in a different manner or attitude than the others.

One of the highest honors for any soldier during the Civil War was the assignment as color-bearer for his unit. But such an honor was also fraught with danger, because the flags drew a high rate of enemy fire in an attempt to shoot down the bearers and perhaps seize the flags as trophies of war.

Flag-bearers thus had to be brave souls. A Union infantry regiment was authorized to carry two flags: a stars and stripes national color and a blue regimental color showing the national eagle. Each flag was inscribed with the number and name of the unit sewn or painted on. Army regulations specified that the color party was to consist of a sergeant and eight corporals, who would protect the flags at all costs.

The infantry colors were large, measuring seventy-two by seventy-eight inches, to ensure that they could be seen on a smoky battlefield and used as rallying points if a regiment became disorganized in combat. Flags were generally made of silk, edged with gold-colored fringe, and had a set of blue and white tassels suspended from the regulation spear-point finial at the top of the nine-foot, ten-inch wooden staff.

The annals of the Civil War are replete with the names of courageous color-bearers and their guards who, in spite of high mortality rates, protected their valued flags. A large portion of the 1,200 Medals of Honor issued during the war were awarded to men who picked up the colors after their bearers were shot down, rescued their flags from enemy hands, or captured Rebel flags in battle.

DR. RICHARD SAUERS

2nd Maryland Infantry, C.S.A., 1864.

DICK AND M. E. CLOW

THUNDER ON LITTLE KENNESAW

From May until June 1864, during the Atlanta Campaign, Confederate general Joseph E. Johnston attempted to lure Maj. Gen. William T. Sherman into attacking him in strong defensive positions, hoping that the Union troops would incur heavy losses and thus reduce Sherman's numerical advantage. Sherman, however, refused to take the bait and repeatedly attempted through flanking movements to cut Johnston's supply line and compel him to fight a major battle on disadvantageous terms.

Finally the two armies confronted each other at the dual peaks of Kennesaw Mountain. Confederate major general Samuel G. French, whose division covered this high eminence, planted twenty guns upon it on about May 24. The road leading to the crest, being difficult to ascend, was exposed to the fire of the Federal batteries on the neighboring heights. After some search, an alternate route was found behind the mountain. A detail of infantry helped the artillerymen with the backbreaking work of hauling the heavy guns up the rugged rocky slope using ropes. To better serve the commanding position, orders were issued to place another battery on Pigeon Hill, a low spur projecting from the southern end of Little Kennesaw. The change of position was issued to Alabama captain Charles L. Lumsden and his battery of four 12-pounder Napoleons.

At 10 A.M. on the command "Fire," the bronze guns thundered. Captain Lumsden ordered, "Load!" as the smell of sulfur and smoke hung in the air. Pvt. Jacob Gurley was thumbing the vent of the number-three gun while a companion swabbed out the bore when fifty-one Federal guns roared in reply. A Parrott shell hurtled through the embrasure and exploded the three caisson chests, scattering live rounds and igniting a tray of fuses with the friction primers. But Lieutenant Hargrove, with coolness and bravery, grabbed a sponge bucket and extinguished the disastrous flames.

General French recorded the following from his position on Little Kennesaw:

> *We sat there perhaps an hour enjoying a bird's eye view of one of the most magnificent sights ever allotted to man, to look down upon a hundred and fifty thousand men arrayed in the strife of battle . . . as the infantry closed in the blue smoke of the musket marked out the line of battle, while over it rose cumuli-like clouds, the white smoke of the artillery. So many were the guns concentrated to silence those guns of ours . . . and so incessant was the roar of cannon and explosion of shells passing over our heads or crashing on the rocks around us, that naught else could be heard; and so, with a roar as constant as Niagara and as sharp as the crash of thunder . . . we sat in silence watching the changing scenes of this great panorama.*

> WILLIAM ERQUITT

ARTIST COMMENTS

A visit to speak before the Atlanta Civil War Roundtable gave me the opportunity to scout the actual location of this battle and take pictures. The battery earthworks still remain, and visiting the site provided a true picture of how high this mountain actually was, with a superb view in every direction. My guide was noted local Civil War historian Bill Erquitt, who knows pretty much every square inch of the hill and battlefield.

A view from Little Kennesaw Mountain during the on-site photo shoot.

SOUTHERN STEEL

In 1864, Gen. Nathan Bedford Forrest was rapidly becoming a living legend. The previous spring, he had run Col. Abel Streight's mule brigade into the ground and captured the whole command with a numerically inferior force. Forrest was bold and aggressive, and in February 1864, Union general William Sooy Smith gave him the opportunity to shine once again.

As part of Maj. Gen. William T. Sherman's Meridian campaign, Smith had moved from his encampments in west Tennessee with 7,000 hand-picked horsemen, with the goal of linking up with Sherman's mainly infantry force and moving to strike at the Confederate industry in east Mississippi and Alabama. The phantom of Forrest began to haunt Smith almost immediately, and he saw imaginary horsemen in every swamp and tree. Convincing himself that he was opposed by too great of a force to overcome, he gave up on his mission and began to retire back to Tennessee.

Forrest then launched his forces on Smith's rear, dogging him in his northward retreat. "Keeping up the Skeer" was a maxim attributed to Forrest, and against Smith he did. At the little village of Okalona, Mississippi, Smith tried to make a stand to stem the pursuit. In his typical manner, Forrest threw his force at the superior Federal command. The assault forced them back in disorder. Amongst the chaos, tragedy struck Forrest when his youngest brother, Col. Jeffrey Forrest, fell dead. Jeffrey had been raised by his brother in a manner more like a son, and his death struck the general hard.

Though overcome with anger and grief, Forrest kept up the fight, recklessly launching himself and his command in savage attacks on the Federal line. Several times he outdistanced his escort and was seen alone, shooting and slashing at the astonished Federal troopers. The ferocity of the attacks drove back the Federals; it seemed that every time they would rally, they were assailed by screaming gray troopers. Smith's forces were beaten and began to retreat anew. Forrest had once again defeated a superior army sent against him and was well on his way to cementing his reputation as the "wizard of the saddle."

LEE WHITE

ARTIST COMMENTS

This was my first work depicting the great warrior Nathan Bedford Forrest. He was a man of action, and I feel that is the best way to paint him. Plenty of other generals read maps and pointed, but few repeatedly engaged in direct hand-to-hand combat. In this painting, most of the models were actually posed on horseback. Famed sculptor James Muir posed for Forrest, and although I posed the upper part of Forrest's torso and head from a dismounted model, western artist Dave Powell posed for at least of the Union cavalrymen. Both were superb riders, and we had an action-packed day at the stables.

It's difficult to stage horses lying the ground or falling. On hot days after the modeling, I follow the animals, which often roll in the dust after the saddle is removed. You have to know the warning signs of when it's coming, as a good tumble lasts only a few moments.

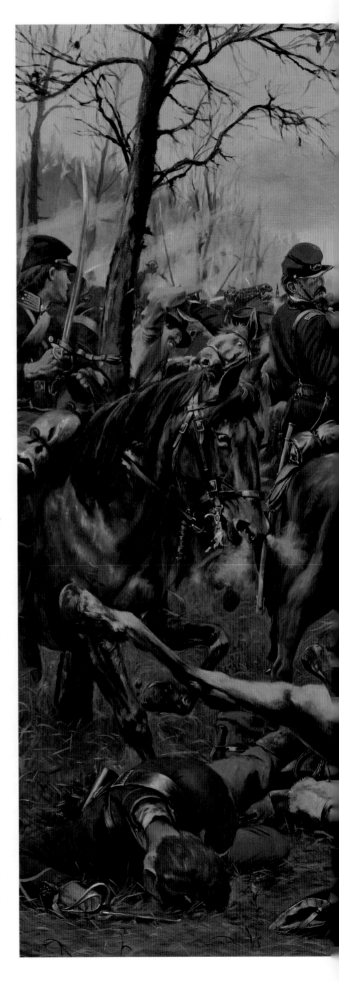

THE GRAY WALL

The Army of Tennessee was the ill-starred force that was charged with the defense of the western Confederacy. Under the leadership of Generals Braxton Bragg, Joseph E. Johnston, and John Bell Hood, the army rarely saw victory; instead, the men saw the lives of their comrades wasted and territory lost, yet they fought on with grim determination even after it had become painfully apparent that their cause was lost. The remnant of the army would not surrender until April 26, 1865, nearly two weeks after the vaunted Army of Northern Virginia had done so.

Historian Thomas Connelly best described the heart of the army: "The Army of Tennessee fought well and left an admirable record. True, it was beaten two out of every three times it took the field. Yet it was this constant defeat which made it a great army. It required something special, and intangible élan, to come back from the humiliation of Missionary Ridge and fight heroically at Kennesaw Mountain." Indeed, that élan enabled the army to see defeat at Atlanta but come back to invade Tennessee and charge at Franklin, to be beaten at Nashville but still be able to take the field one last time at Bentonville.

It could be said that the Army of Tennessee was a true "Band of Brothers," as their élan did not come from great leadership of generals like Robert E. Lee. Instead, it was from each other that the men drew their fighting spirit. And it was that spirit that enabled it to withstand nearly constant defeat but be able to come back to fight again.

LEE WHITE

ARTIST COMMENTS

At the time I made this painting, I had not done much with specific subjects, as dealers were apprehensive that they might not sell well. Nevertheless, I decided here to concentrate on the private soldiers, which I find an enjoyable challenge. Every character should look like sombody you might know, not a group of vapid generic faces. The visual contrast between gritty old veterans and fresh young recruits gives a painting more credibility.

The hunt for great character types is always a priority. My wife, Donna, has gone up to great candidates on the street or in the supermarket line and asked them to pose. Surprisingly, most actually do. We eventually started running ads for models in the local paper, which also brought us many great faces. These people have loyally posed for years and have become great friends.

Private, 20th Tennessee Infantry, C.S.A., 1863.

PAUL SCHIERL

Rebel Yell

Since the time when three Roman legions disappeared within the Teutenberg Forest of Germany, generals have tried to avoid fighting in forests. On September 19–20, 1863, Gen. Braxton Bragg and Gen. William S. Rosecrans fought a battle that neither wanted in the thickets and glades of Chickamauga. It was a soldiers' battle, as the generals frequently lost control of the fighting in the shadows of the great oaks and chestnuts that thrived there. The Rebel yell echoed among the trees, a sound that one Confederate described as "that do or die expression, that maniacal maelstrom of sound; that penetrating, rasping, shrieking, blood curling noise that could be heard for miles and whose volume reached the heavens—such an expression as never yet came from the throats of sane men, but from men whom the seething blast of imaginary hell would not check while the sound lasted."

The Union line grudgingly fell back as it was battered by the Confederates, and disaster finally struck when a gap was accidentally created in the Union line at the moment that Gen. James Longstreet attacked. The right wing of the Union army collapsed and was sent flying from the field, leaving a small force to hold out until sunset under the leadership of Gen. George H. Thomas, who later became known as the Rock of Chickamauga. Ambrose Bierce, then a young staff officer, later recalled hearing a great Rebel yell as they left the field that night:

> At last it grew too dark to fight. Then away to our left and rear some of Bragg's people set up "the rebel yell." It was taken up successively and passed round to our front, along our right and behind us again, and it seemed almost to have got to the point whence it started. It was the ugliest sound that any mortal ever heard—even a mortal exhausted and unnerved by two days of hard fighting, without sleep, without rest, without food, and without hope. There was, however, a space somewhere at the back of us across which that horrible yell did not prolong—and through that we finally returned in profound silence and dejection unmolested.

LEE WHITE

NATHAN BEDFORD FORREST

From a rural Tennessee background with a backwoods education, Nathan Bedford Forrest became one of the greatest generals produced by either side during the Civil War. He was the only man, North or South, to rise from the rank of private to lieutenant general. By the later part of 1864, he had reached the height of his success, having defeated numerically superior forces that had been sent to destroy him, captured U.S. naval vessels, and stormed the streets of Federally controlled Memphis. He became such a threat to Gen. William T. Sherman's supply lines that the Union general had labeled him the very devil and ordered commanders to "follow Forrest to the death if it costs 10,000 lives and breaks the Treasury, there will never be peace in Tennessee till Forrest is dead."

It was at this time that Forrest was called on to support Gen. John Bell Hood in his campaign into Tennessee in the autumn of 1864. Forrest was charged with covering Hood's advance, which he did with his usual aggressiveness, clashing with Federal troops as they moved into the state. Forrest and his troopers fought desperately at Spring Hill and the bloody battle of Franklin before arriving at Nashville. There Hood detached Forrest to strike at the "railroad, blockhouses, and telegraph lines leading from Nashville to Murfreesborough." Forrest was once again in his element as he seized and destroyed blockhouses, captured trains, wrecked tracks and burned bridges. He then received orders to strike the large Federal garrison at Murfreesboro. As he moved on the garrison he was joined first by Gen. William Bates's division of infantry, and then by two more infantry brigades. While Forrest's command closed in on the town on December 6, Federal infantry marched out to meet him.

The battle that followed went against Forrest, as his infantry broke and ran, much to his disgust. Forrest was forced to pull back, but he continued

Confederate States Marines.

U.S. Marines.

to operate against the railroad until he received word on December 16 of the disaster that had befallen Hood, along with orders to rejoin Hood on the general's retreat back to Alabama. In the nightmarish winter retreat from Tennessee, Forrest's skill never shone brighter as he parried attacks, set ambushes, and slowed the Federal pursuit enough to allow the defeated Confederates to limp back to the safety of the Tennessee River.

LEE WHITE

ARTIST COMMENTS

For some time, I had been getting requests for another Nathan Bedford Forrest painting, depicting him in action,

and also a winter scene. Why not combine both in one painting? Not portraying a specific episode gave me much more latitude in design.

I usually paint snow by doing an underpainting with thick white oil and working in textures with a stiff-bristle brush. Snow is not just white or gray; it picks up an abundance of other colors from the sky, whether in clouds or sunlight. So after the white paint dries for several days, I apply thin blue, pink, and brownish washes where they are needed, mostly in the shadowy areas. After further drying, I partially paint over the color tints with a thin white opaque layer to highlight the light areas. When all is dry, I add the final details.

"Put the Boys In"

In the spring of 1864, Gen. Ulysses S. Grant was determined to bring military pressure to all sides of the Confederacy to stretch and perhaps break the South's ability to respond to Union action. He sent the German-born Maj. Gen. Franz Sigel and an army of roughly 9,000 to take control of the Shenandoah Valley, known as "the breadbasket of the Confederacy."

Gen. John C. Breckinridge moved rapidly to counter Sigel, picking up every available home guard and stray unit. Passing through Lexington, he sent an urgent dispatch to the Virginia Military Institute (VMI) that he needed its entire Cadet Corps. Early on the morning of May 11, a group of 257 cadets prepared to join Breckinridge's army of roughly 5,300 combined arms. Another 30 cadets brought two 3-inch artillery rifles.

Some of the cadets had already experienced war firsthand. Oliver Perry Evans, a private in the 22nd Virginia, carried the flag, and George Raum also had served in the Confederate army. But these cadets were the exceptions. Though most were young, with Lewis Davis having just turned fifteen, all were ready to prove their worth in battle. Breckinridge, however, planned to have the cadets guard the wagon train, freeing up veterans to do the fighting.

After light skirmishing on May 14, it was obvious to even the young cadets that the next day would bring the big fight. As morning dawned, less than a mile separated the two armies. The cadets were placed in the second line as reserves, just in case.

By noon, the Federal line had drawn up about a mile north of town, along a ridge running east to west on the Jacob Bushong farm. A line of twenty cannons protected Sigel's infantry. It was a formidable position anchored on the east by cavalry along the Valley Turnpike and on the west by a 200-foot cliff overlooking the Shenandoah River.

The Confederates advanced around the farmhouse and into the orchard, pausing along a split-rail fence that separated it from a wheatfield just as rain began pouring down. Although they could not see through the rain and smoke of battle, the Federal artillerymen loaded double canister and blasted away at the gray-clad soldiers, blowing a large and threatening gap into the center of the Confederate line. Breckinridge realized he had to plug the gap or risk being driven off the field, but the ethical situation gave him pause: The reserves closest at hand were the VMI cadets. The Confederate commander hesitated to issue the order that appeared to be his only hope of saving his position. But the moment of defeat or victory had come, and he at last shouted, "Put the boys in, and may God forgive me for the Order!"

The cadets witnessed the devastation just to their front, and then moved from their position near the farmhouse into the orchard. They stepped over the mangled and dying bodies of the veteran soldiers to reach the split-rail fence. Earlier, Union artillery had ripped through the cadet ranks. Now the blue-clad infantrymen sighted on the young cadets.

Sigel quickly ordered his infantry forward to charge the broken Confederate line. But in the confusion of the moment, only the 34th Massachusetts struggled out across the muddy wheatfield, heading right for the hole in the center of the gray line. As the troops neared, the cadets met and repulsed their advance. The Massachusetts regiment reeled back, and the entire Confederate line rose and moved forward. Sigel shouted for the Union line to fall back, but before all the guns of the 30th New York battery could be limbered, the cadets were upon them. They swarmed around their great prize as Oliver Evans mounted the gun and furiously waved the bullet-riddled flag of the Cadet Corps.

Breckinridge pursued the Union army to the banks of the Shenandoah River, but Sigel made good his escape. As the Confederate general passed the mud-clad and bloody cadets, he shouted, "Well done Virginians, well done men!"

But the victory had come at a great price: Ten cadets were dead or dying; another forty-seven were wounded—over 24 percent casualties. The cadets' actions that day remain a unique moment in American history. Never before or since has an entire student body engaged in pitched combat with such casualties.

KEITH GIBSON

ARTIST COMMENTS

This painting entailed rounding up a large, diverse group of teenage boys to model for the cadets. Happily, my beautiful niece Jessica was easily able to recruit the required male cannon fodder at her high school. They were new at modeling, and it took a good bit of acting lessons to get them into the drama of the moment, but with practice they did quite well. Being less self-conscious, younger models often strike more candid and energetic poses.

Canteen posed in a mud puddle for "Put the Boys In."

The Bushong house and grounds are owned by VMI, which maintains very closely its wartime appearance. In examining period photos of the main house, I noticed that some details, such as the dark trim on the shutters, were different at the time of the battle, and I incorporated them into the painting. VMI runs an excellent museum on the grounds that is well worth a visit.

I spent more than three months on this painting, which is very large, at fifty by eighty inches. The house alone took several days. Many times I had to stop work in one section to allow the paint to dry before adding further detail.

MAHONE'S COUNTERATTACK

When the Yankees blew a hole in the Confederate line at Petersburg, Virginia, on July 30, 1864, one of the first things Gen. Robert E. Lee did was order Brig. Gen. William Mahone, commander of the division manning the right flank of the Army of Northern Virginia's line, to send two brigades to reinforce the lines behind the Crater.

Mahone's brigades arrived on the scene, and sometime after 9 A.M., his old brigade of Virginians, now led by Col. David Weisiger, launched an assault on the Yankees north of the Crater. By this time, soldiers from both the 1st and 2nd Divisions of the IX Corps were manning the trenches, with the regiments and brigades all mixed up. Just before Mahone's arrival, the 4th Division of the IX Corps, composed of African-American soldiers, was preparing to launch an attack when the Virginians slammed into them, hurling them back into the packed trenches. Lt. Col. John Bross of the 29th U.S. Colored Troops, with his flag in hand, was killed as the Rebels surged forward. Men were so closely jammed together that many could not even raise their muskets to fire at the approaching Virginians. The Southerners were eager to fight and became enraged when they saw black soldiers in front of them.

Even though Weisiger's men managed to retake most of the trenches north of the Crater, they were not strong enough to push on into the Crater itself. But they had negated an important Union attack and regained the initiative.

DR. RICHARD SAUERS

ARTIST COMMENTS

Working as a consultant with historians Brian Pohanka and Michael Kraus on the *Cold Mountain* film kindled my interest in this often over-looked but fascinating battle. My role was to guide the costumers and prop makers, who did a very good job as a whole. I think in those areas, there has never been a more accurate Civil War feature film. Between us, we managed to change the entire look of the final production from what had been previously scripted. Brian, Mike, and I went on location to Romania and did yeoman service during months of filming in the sweltering countryside, with more than 1,000 extras who had to be dressed every morning. About half of the battle and hospital scenes that we worked so hard on were cut and never made it to the screen. Some of the great Massachusetts battle flags that were re-created sadly never showed up in the final version.

I used four terrific local African Americans for all the U.S. Colored Troops in this painting. Usually I try to have a greater number of models, but because I was depicting the backs of heads in many cases, I used each of them several times with slight changes. The model for the color-bearer came up with his own dramatic positioning and great determined facial expression. Many of the most realistic poses have been unplanned. Often I've attempted to get a model to adopt a candid stance only to have him stiffen up and look awful. Then, when my back is turned and the camera and pressure are off, he relaxes and there it is—perfection.

WILLIAM GLADSTONE

DeGress's Battery

The big gun roared. Seventeen seconds later, and two-and-a-half miles away, a bullet-shaped shell exploded at the intersection of Ellis and Ivy Streets, mortally wounding a small child. It was 1 P.M., July 20, 1864. The siege of Atlanta had begun.

That same afternoon, Confederate general John Bell Hood's outnumbered Army of Tennessee pitched into the approaching Union troops at Peachtree Creek. The fierce fighting failed to loosen Maj. Gen. William T. Sherman's tightening grip on Atlanta, but Hood resolved to attack again, this time to the east, where his West Point classmate Maj. Gen. James B. McPherson had closed within cannon shot of the city.

On the evening of July 21, Hood sent Lt. Gen. William J. Hardee's corps marching south to strike the unprotected left flank and rear of McPherson's Army of the Tennessee. After an exhausting all-night march of fifteen miles, Hardee's infantry burst from the woods with a wild yell shortly after noon on July 22, expecting to see the backs of McPherson's men. Instead, they found themselves facing two small divisions of Maj. Gen. Grenville M. Dodge's XVI Corps.

On the left of Dodge's thin blue line, the 66th Illinois Infantry—the Western Sharpshooters—began blazing away with their brass-framed, lever-action Henry rifles, each man pumping out sixteen rounds before pausing to reload. McPherson watched the struggle for a few minutes before spurring away to bring up reinforcements. He had not gone far when a Rebel skirmisher shot him dead.

Visibly shaken when he learned of McPherson's death, Sherman ordered Maj. Gen. John A. Logan to take command of the hard-pressed Army of the Tennessee. As Logan's men fought desperately to hold their ground, Hood landed another heavy blow. About 4 P.M., Maj. Gen. Benjamin F. Cheatham's corps breached the Union trenches just north of the Georgia Railroad and swarmed past the Troup Hurt house, an unfinished two-story brick mansion.

Capt. Francis DeGress, commanding Battery H, 1st Illinois Light Artillery, saw the oncoming Confederates rout his supporting infantry. Realizing his battery, which had hurled the first Yankee shells into Atlanta, would soon be overrun, he had his four 20-pounder Parrott guns spiked with 20-penny nails. "Every man look out for himself," he yelled.

As the battle's outcome trembled in the balance, "Black Jack" Logan rode up to General Dodge. "I want one of your best brigades as quick as God almighty will let you," he said.

Dodge summoned Col. August Mersy. His three regiments shouldered their rifles and knapsacks and double-quicked after Logan in the sweltering heat. Met by scattered shots as they reached the railroad and turned left, Capt. William S. Boyd, commanding the 66th Illinois, ordered his regiment's bullet-riddled battle flag unfurled. As the colors hurried past, Logan, sitting astride his sweating black steed, waved his hat and yelled, "Yes, boys, in the name of the eternal God, let the old flag wave."

The men answered with three hearty cheers. They had gone about a mile and half when heavy fire halted them, panting and breathless, behind the railroad embankment. Colonel Mersy's horse reared and fell dead across a plank fence. A soldier who pulled the colonel from under his fallen mount asked if he was hurt. "Shust shot in de leg a leedle," Mersy replied in his thick German accent.

Charles Smithcall's 20-pound Parrot rifle.

Turning command over to Lt. Col. Robert N. Adams of the 81st Ohio, Mersy told him to drive the Rebels back and have every man yell "so loud what he can."

The command "Double-quick, charge!" echoed down the line. Yelling like banshees, the brigade surged over the tracks, the 12th Illinois on the left, the 81st Ohio in the center, and the 66th Illinois on the right, driving everything before them. At the same time, Logan urged even more troops toward the captured guns.

The 66th Illinois and 81st Ohio arrived first. Assisted by some of DeGress's artillerymen, they unspiked the guns and fired at the retreating Rebels. The number four gun exploded on the third round, but Captain DeGress was just glad to get his battery back. Tearfully grasping Colonel Adams's hand, he said, "I want to thank you and your brigade for what you have done."

DAVID EVANS

ALLATOONA PASS

Atlanta had fallen. After six weeks of siege and shelling, the beleaguered city had surrendered to Maj. Gen. William T. Sherman. The triumphant Union troops who marched in on September 2, 1864, were expecting a well-earned rest, but Confederate general John B. Hood had other ideas. On September 29, he led his battered, badly outnumbered Army of Tennessee across the Chattahoochee River thirty miles below Atlanta, and marched northward. After cutting the railroad that Sherman depended on for supplies, Hood intended to lure him back into the north Georgia mountains, defeat him in battle, and regain the Confederate territory lost that summer.

Hood's troops reached the Western and Atlantic Railroad at Big Shanty on October 3 and began tearing up track. The next day, Maj. Gen. Samuel G. French's division received orders to move twelve miles northwest to fill up the 360-foot railroad cut at Allatoona Pass and burn the trestle over the Etowah River. Sherman had already left Atlanta and hurried after Hood, but the broken and burned tracks at Big Shanty made it impossible to continue the pursuit by rail. The telegraph was down too. That afternoon, red and white signal flags fluttering from the rocky crest of Kennesaw Mountain wigwagged a message over the head of Hood's army, directing Brig. Gen. John M. Corse to move forward with his entire command. Corse's division of the hard-fighting XV Corps was at Rome, thirty-five miles northwest of Allatoona. Recent rains had washed out several sections of the railroad, leaving Corse with only enough rolling stock to move about 1,100 men from Col. Richard Rowett's brigade. As Rowett's men crowded into the cars, a junior officer asked about

where to put provisions. "Hell," Corse growled, "we are not going to eat; we are going to fight." Corse's train chugged into Allatoona shortly after midnight.

Just before dawn, Rebel artillery opened fire. After an hour-long bombardment, French sent a note demanding Allatoona's surrender to avoid "the needless effusion of blood." "General French must either be a fool, or else he thinks somebody else is," Corse observed as he scrawled a defiant reply. Unaware that Corse had reinforced the little Union garrison, French formed Brig. Gen. Francis M. Cockrell's Missouri Brigade west of the railroad, supported by Brig. Gen. William H. Young's Texans and North Carolinians. About 9 A.M., they advanced. Cockrell's skirmishers quickly routed the 93rd Illinois Infantry from some outlying trenches and rifle pits.

Rowett's 7th Illinois and 39th Iowa Infantries waited behind a small redoubt straddling the Cartersville Road. The Iowans carried muzzle-loading Springfields, but each of the Illinois men had paid $51 for a Model 1860 Henry repeater.

Met by a staggering hail of lead, Cockrell's front ranks fell to the ground and spent the next hour clearing paths through the barricading limbs and branches. Then, joined by Young's brigade, they sprang forward again. Rifle and artillery fire riddled the Rebel ranks. Then two regiments of Brig. Gen. Claudius W. Sears's Mississippi Brigade struck the 39th Iowa's right flank, sweeping it away like chaff. At the same time, a rush of Rebel butternut and gray surged over Rowett's redoubt. "John, go for those colors," Capt. Joseph Boyce yelled. Sgt. John Ragland of the 1st Missouri Infantry grabbed the 39th Iowa's flag and ripped the Stars and Stripes from its

Henry rifle used by a soldier of the 66th Illinois during the Atlanta campaign. TROIANI COLLECTION

staff just as Boyce hurled a dirt clod that struck the Yankee color-bearer right between the eyes. Others fought with rifle butts, bayonets, and bullets at point-blank range. In some places, the ground literally ran red with blood before the Union line finally broke.

By 11 A.M., French had driven Corse's entire command into two small forts perched on either side of the railroad. "Hold Allatoona," Sherman signaled the defenders. "I will help you." Sherman's message later inspired Philip P. Bliss to write the popular hymn, "Hold the Fort for I Am Coming," and Corse's men did hold, but at a fearful cost. By the time a shortage of ammunition finally forced French to withdraw, a third of the men on both sides lay dead or wounded.

DR. DAVID EVANS

Working with models for "Allatoona Pass."

Cutting tree stumps with a hand axe for Allatoona Pass.

ARTIST COMMENTS

Noted historians David Evans and Bill Scaife took pictures for me on the actual site and provided invaluable research. Despite that, this scene was tough to re-create because the hill, cleared at the time of the battle, today is covered with dense woods.

Originally I had posed the crew hauling off the entire Napoleon gun and limber. The models spent many hours dragging the original 2,000-pound gun across my driveway on a sweltering summer day. But when I started sketching in the painting, it became clear that I had posed much more than would fit on the canvas. Showing the entire party with the gun would have meant a more panoramic scene with smaller figures, which would have diminished the drama, so sadly they had to go.

The original fifty-by-eighty-inch painting is on display at the new Booth Museum of Western Art in Cartersville, Georgia.

MAJOR GENERAL PATRICK CLEBURNE

ARTIST COMMENTS

Like Forrest, Cleburne is one of the more interesting Civil War figures to paint. With his chiseled and scarred face with great cheekbones, he had a hardened soldier's visage that is an artist's dream. Here I decided to show the moment before his horse was shot and he was compelled to proceed on foot. Working at a local stable, I spent a late afternoon photographing an expert rider on a great horse taking jumps over a low fence. Back at the house, another model who looked similar to the general was posed on a saddle stand setup that approximated the best horse photo. Using the same lighting, I was able to come up with an action pose that I felt would dominate the picture.

I applied a thin red wash to the entire underdrawing, which gave the warmth of evening glow to the scene. This tint shows through in many areas, which increases the effect.

Hardee flag made by the artist's wife in the early 1980s.

OPDYCKE'S TIGERS

"The air of the November evening was cool and bracing, the sun shone brightly, and the clouds were pink in the western sky. For a few moments there was not a sound except the sturdy tramp of the men in beautiful alignment and the cautionary orders of the company officers." This is how a Confederate captain described the beginning of the tragic battle of Franklin, Tennessee.

Confederate general John Bell Hood was desperate to defeat his old West Point friend, John Schofield, as he surveyed the Federal entrenchments that ringed the town of Franklin. In his mind, there was only one option—a frontal attack, the same desperate tactic that had won him laurels in Virginia. Around 4 P.M., he ordered the two Corps of his army that were present to make the attack.

As the Confederates marched across the field in fine array, the men of Gen. George Wagner's division looked on in disbelief. They had been placed in advance of the main fortified line and now knew something was very wrong. They received no orders to fall back and soon found themselves confronted with a tidal wave of gray and brown. In the face of such overwhelming odds, they broke for the safety of the main line with the howling Confederates hot on their heels.

As they approached the main line, the Federals there held their fire as Wagner's men made a human shield for the Confederates. Finally, before it was too late, the main line delivered a devastating volley, bringing down men of both sides. In the Federal center, the Confederates were still able to overrun their entrenchments and break their line. It appeared that Hood's desperate gamble might work, as the gray-clad soldiers spilled through the gap and onto the grounds of the home of Fountain Branch Carter.

As the fugitives of Wagner's division streamed to the rear they drew the attention of Col. Emerson Opdycke. Opdycke was the commander of another of Wagner's brigades, but on seeing the exposed position he was to occupy, he had ignored his orders and marched on into Franklin, where he rested his weary men. He quickly ordered his men into line and rushed them with a yell into the surprised and exhausted Confederates around the Carter house. The fighting there was desperate and hand-to-hand. Opdycke and his old regiment, the 125th Ohio, fought among the outbuildings of the home. Soon the ground was slick with blood and covered with bodies, as Opdycke and his Tigers were able to seal the breach in the Federal lines and end the only opportunity that Hood had of winning the battle.

In the aftermath of the battle, thirteen Confederate generals were found among the casualties, five of them dead, including the pride of the army, Patrick Cleburne. Many regimental commanders and company commanders were gone as well. Hood had sacrificed his army on his desperate bet, and though he held the ground, Schofield was able to march his men back to Nashville and the safety of its massive forts. Hood would soon follow.

LEE WHITE

ARTIST COMMENTS

It seems that every time I decide on a battle scene to paint, the background is just a tree line or something else equally monotonous. The chance to paint something in a backyard of an interesting brick house was a rarity indeed. Pictures were taken at the Carter house, which is a wonderful restoration. Only the original configuration of stepped roof line had to be re-created and a few other minor details added. To give the appearance of a typical nineteenth-century backyard and garden, I added broken flower pots and other sundry items.

THE FORLORN HOPE

The 1864 Overland campaign in Virginia tested the endurance of soldiers in both armies. Week by week, battle after battle, the stamina and efficiency of the fighting men eroded under the pressure of constant action. The best evidence of that decline came in mid June, when the exhausted armies stood before Petersburg. Several days of botched attacks east of the city had aroused frustration among the Federal generals. Army commander George Meade issued increasingly waspish orders to his subordinates, vainly hoping to forge an offensive combination that would crack the Confederate defenses before the armies fell into a full-blown siege.

The II Corps of Meade's army had been a reliable force for three years, but staggering losses during the campaign had shattered the corps' effectiveness. Now Meade called on the hulk of this once great formation. His last major presiege attack came on the afternoon of June 18, 1864. Its failure would be historic. Untested regiments began filling manpower gaps in Meade's army by Spotsylvania in the second week of May. Heavy artillery units, most of them fresh from the defenses of Washington and armed with rifles rather than cannons, merged with grimy veterans to form incongruous infantry brigades. At Spotsylvania, Totopotomoy Creek, and especially Cold Harbor, the heavy artillerists absorbed shocking losses. Brigade commanders continued to feed the large new regiments into the fray.

The 1st Maine Heavy Artillery had shed its inexperience at Spotsylvania and numbered no more than 900 soldiers by the time it reached Petersburg. The men had seen enough of the war by June 18 to realize that a frontal assault against the Confederate defenses near the Hare house could be disastrous. As part of Col. Daniel Chaplin's brigade, the Maine heavies marched up to the Prince George Court House Road in preparation for a direct attack. As that new position brought the regiment closer to the enemy lines, one of the men wrote later, "we knew what was up with us."

The unit formed a triple line of battle before stepping out into the treeless fields in front of the Confederate entrenchments. Other brigades of Mott's division eyed similar terrain. When the order came, the whole mass moved into the attack—"a grand charge or Slaughter as you may have it." Soon many of the veteran regiments fell away, their taste for such things ruined by their experiences earlier in the campaign. Determined to persevere, the Maine artillerists pushed ahead into a converging fire. "The earth was literally torn up with iron and lead," wrote a survivor. "The field became a burning, seething, crashing, hissing hell, in which human courage, flesh, and bone were struggling with an impossibility."

The blue-clad attackers retreated to safety and counted their losses. In about ten minutes of action, the 1st Maine Heavy Artillery had lost approximately 625 men. Civil War numbers and losses are difficult to figure with complete accuracy, but most calculations agree that no regiment in either army lost as many men in a single battle as did this one in its disastrous 600 seconds outside of Petersburg.

ROBERT E. L. KRICK

ARTIST COMMENTS
Depecting figures at a full run has been a problem for artists of all eras. Most of the models for this effort were posed while running, which involved an afternoon of exhausting passes by the camera. I selected the best poses for use, many of which I then altered in the painting process to create the feel of even more action. The several figures on the far left whose legs are not seen were posed stationary to allow me to concentrate on the facial expressions with more detail. The realistic pose of the officer never could have been achieved any other way than by actually having him run.

Model takes a fall during shooting for "The Forlorn Hope."

FORWARD THE COLORS

ARTIST COMMENTS

This picture was inspired by a painting I saw as a youngster of French Revolutionary troops advancing with an extremely attractive, scantily clad female color-bearer. I don't recall where or when I saw it, but for some reason the image became permanently affixed in my subconscious. Ron Tunison posed for the officer, and Donna made the flag for him to pose with. To get a good bullet-torn effect with this great 2nd National flag, I washed it several times, dragged it around outside, and then fired some bullets through it. Undignified treatment, sadly, but the only way to show it in its war-torn glory. Soldierly type that Ron is, only a few takes were needed. All pictures were great, and it was difficult to select the best one.

The flag that Donna made.

Projected version of "Forward the Colors"— posed but never used. Maybe someday in the future!

Medal of Honor

PAMPLIN PARK

Recent Union successes southwest of Petersburg had culminated in the capture of the strategically important intersection called Five Forks on April 1, 1865. Grant assumed that Lee would reinforce the area in order to protect the South Side Railroad, his only remaining supply line into Petersburg. The Union commander decided to order a massive attack across the entire Confederate front at dawn the next day to exploit any weakness created by Lee's shifting troops.

The battle-tested VI Corps, at this time the premier fighting corps in the Army of the Potomac, drew the assignment to assault a one-mile section of Confederate works six miles southwest of Petersburg, defended by three determined but badly outnumbered Confederate brigades from Georgia and North Carolina.

At 4:40 A.M., some 14,000 men of the VI Corps, an attack formation larger than the Pickett-Pettigrew Charge at Gettysburg, advanced in a wedge-shaped formation. Ahead, through a thin picket line and multiple rows of imposing abatis, lay powerful Confederate entrenchments, described by one Union officer as "the strongest line of earthworks ever constructed in North America."

At the apex of the VI Corps wedge was the Vermont Brigade, and in its front ranks was the 5th Vermont Infantry. Among its line officers was a beardless twenty-year-old captain, Charles G. Gould, who had risen through the ranks to become his company's commander. At the forefront of his unit, Gould pushed his way through the entanglements, shouting encouragement to his men as artillery fire blasted the advancing ranks. The shattered formations surged forward in the predawn gloom, drifting dangerously to the right to avoid the deadly canister. Shouted orders from the rear directed the lead companies to move to the left in order to avoid collisions with other Federal formations.

Gould by crossing the ravine that guided his company and approaching the Confederate line in a direction that isolated him from the rest of his regiment. Finding himself trapped between approaching Federal troops to his rear and the relentless fire of the 37th North Carolina Infantry in his front, Gould opted to push forward, the battlefield illuminated by the strobe of muzzle and cannon blasts. Descending into the moat and scrambling up the steep slope of the Confederate works, Gould emerged alone atop the enemy fortifications. The young captain described what happened next:

My appearance on the parapet was met with a leveled musket, which fortunately missed fire. I immediately jumped into the work, and my part in the engagement was soon over. I was scarcely inside before a bayonet was thrust through my face and a sword-thrust returned for it that fully repaid the wound given me, as I was subsequently informed that it killed my assailant. At almost the same breath an officer—or some one armed with a sword—gave me a severe cut in the head. The remainder of my brief stay in the work was a confused scramble, from which, had my assailants been fewer in number, I should scarcely have escaped. As it was, firing on their part would have been dangerous for their own men; consequently their efforts were apparently restricted to the use of bayonets and clubbed muskets. During the struggle I was once seized and my overcoat partially pulled off, and probably at this time another bayonet wound was given me in the back, as the bayonet passed through my inner coat between the shoulders, while my overcoat remained intact. This was the most severe wound of the three, the bayonet entering the spine and penetrating nearly to the spinal cord. I have no distinct recollection of what followed, until I found myself at the parapet, trying to climb out of the work, but unable to do so. At this time, Private Henry H. Recor, Company A, Fifth Vermont, appeared upon the parapet at that point. The brave fellow recognized the situation, and notwithstanding the danger incurred in doing so, pulled me upon the parapet, receiving a gunshot wound himself while saving me.

Capt. Charles G. Gould is credited with being the first man of the VI Corps over the Confederate works on April 2, 1865, an act that earned him the Medal of Honor.

A. Wilson Greene

ARTIST COMMENTS

When Will Greene at Pamplin Park approached me about doing this painting, I cringed at the thought of another night scene. Even the participants had commented at the time about the extremely dark night, so I knew this would be a tough one, especially with the hero in a dark uniform to boot. The only light source that night had been the musket flashes, which I used to illuminate Captain Gould, with the aid of some extra floodlights shone on the model from the direction of the gunfire.

About fifteen years ago, I had bought Gould's coat, cape, and underwear from a New England antique dealer without even realizing who he was. I finally did some research after having them for a while, and it became apparent what an interesting set I had aquired. It is now on loan and display at Pamplin Park near Petersburg, Virginia.

SOLDIERS' TRIBUTE

Having surrendered the Army of Northern Virginia, Gen. Robert E. Lee rode back toward his headquarters tent through a cool and dark Palm Sunday evening. The sun behind the clouds slanted near the horizon; sunset in Richmond that night came at 6:24. A chaplain present with the army described the weather: "The morning had been bright and fair. By noon dark and gloomy clouds had gathered over the whole face of the sky."

From a distance of half a mile, Gen. Edward Porter Alexander saw Lee coming out of the village on his familiar gray horse, Traveller, at about 4:30 P.M. Lt. Col. Charles Mar-

shall, Lee's reliable thirty-four-year-old aide, rode beside his chief. "A strong desire seized me," Alexander wrote, "to have the men do something, to indicate to the general that our affection for him was even deeper than in the days of greatest victory & prosperity." Under orders from Alexander and his subordinate officers, artillerymen hurried to the roadside and formed into line. Alexander instructed them "to uncover their heads, but in silence," as Lee passed.

The hastily formed plan for a dignified, if emotional, tribute to the surrendered army's chieftain fell apart at once. Infantry posted nearby swarmed around the artillerists and as

Lee drew nigh, someone began cheering and the others joined in. When he could be heard, the general "told the men in a few words that he had done his best for them & advised them to go home & become as good citizens as they had been soldiers." During General Lee's short, simple remarks, "a wave of emotion seemed to strike the crowd & a great many men were weeping." Soldiers pressed close to touch the general or his mount, "to try & express in some way," General Alexander wrote, "the feelings which shook every heart."

A South Carolina surgeon who had served under Lee for most of the war described the moment in a letter to his wife: "I heard some of our men yelling, and saw General Lee and his staff riding towards us, and as he stopped . . . the men crowded around him to shake his hand and every man was shedding tears." Another man observed similarly, "The men flocked round General Lee . . . and met him with shouts and tears." A North Carolinian standing along the road near the Courthouse left a vivid description of the event: "As he approached we could see the reins hanging loose on his horse's neck and his head was sunk on his breast. As the men began to cheer, he raised his head and hat in hand passed by, his face flushed and his eyes ablaze."

Pvt. John Mathews Brown had been attending Washington College in Lexington, Virginia, when war erupted. In March 1862, two weeks after his seventeenth birthday, he enlisted in the Rockbridge Artillery. Brown served steadily with that renowned battery, except when absent sick and while recovering from a wound he had suffered at Malvern Hill.

At Appomattox on the evening of April 9, 1865, Brown went to the edge of the road when he heard a commotion and saw Lee riding through a dense crowd of soldiers. The general stopped in the midst of the throng and spoke briefly, out of Brown's hearing. Someone later told the Rockbridge gunner that Lee had admonished the men that "the bravest and best thing you can do is to go to that wife who is waiting anxiously for you." Then, "as he approached where I stood," Brown recalled, "every head was bared. . . . General Lee's eyes were full of tears, as he turned his face from side to side and looked on the bowed heads of his men."

The next morning, Colonel Marshall found some privacy in General Lee's ambulance, with an orderly posted to deflect interruptions, and drafted in pencil one of the most famous documents in American military history. General Order No. 9, signed by Lee, began: "After four years of arduous service marked by unsurpassed courage and fortitude the Army of Northern Virginia has been compelled to yield to overwhelming numbers and resources."

ROBERT K. KRICK

ARTIST COMMENTS

Europeans have always had a plethora of military painters covering every aspect of practically every important event, but the great moments of American military history have remained virtually unpainted. Had this event happened in France or Germany, there would be dozens of versions of this by all the prominent historical painters. Though this was one of the most stirring moments of the war, it had received only perfunctory treatment without the benefit of serious research.

I posed this painting over a period of one year. As models finished posing projects, I posed each of them for a few more figures in this one. Because this was an overcast scene, lighting was not much of a problem, and I was able to photograph all of the models in the shade. In this way, I wound up incorporating quite a few interesting character types, some of whom live on the West Coast and are rarely available to me.

THE LAST SALUTE

April 12, 1865, was set aside by the Northern authorities at Appomattox Court House as the day for a formal surrender ceremony. Three days earlier, Gen. Robert E. Lee had surrendered the remnants of the Army of Northern Virginia to Ulysses S. Grant in the home of Wilmer McLean. It was agreed that Lee's men would be paroled and allowed to return to their homes. Officers could keep their swords, sidearms, and personal baggage; those with horses could also retain them. One concession was that "the arms, artillery, and public property [were] to be parked and stacked, and turned over to the officers appointed by [Grant] to receive them."

The man given this important task was thirty-seven-year-old Gen. Joshua L. Chamberlain of Maine. Hero at Gettysburg, for which he won the Medal of Honor, and seriously wounded at Petersburg, he was now commanding a brigade in Gen. Charles Griffin's V Corps. Grant instructed him to keep the surrender ceremony simple and do nothing "to humiliate the manhood of the Southern soldiers."

On the chilly gray morning of the twelfth, which eventually became rainy, Chamberlain assembled his old 3rd Brigade. The men lined up parallel to the Richmond-Lynchburg Stage Road, which ran through the county seat village. Supporting them were the other two brigades of Bartlett's 1st Division.

Leading the gray infantry column was thirty-three-year-old Georgia general John B. Gordon. As he rode up to the right of the 3rd Brigade line, the sound of a bugle was heard, and the Union troops snapped into the marching salute (carry arms) to their former enemy. Seeing this, Gordon quickly caught the spirit and straightened himself in his saddle, dropping his sword tip to the toe of his boot in salutation to Chamberlain and his men. He then ordered his soldiers to return the Union salute.

Chamberlain was positioned at the right of the line, next to the 32nd Massachusetts. He and his mounted staff officers were marked by their division flag, with a red maltese cross on a field of white with a blue border.

The Confederate soldiers filed between the Northern ranks, then turned and faced their old opponents, dressing their line. On command, they fixed bayonets, stepped forward, and stacked arms, then laid down their accoutrements. Finally, and many times in tears, they rendered their battle flags. These men wept unashamedly in front of their for-

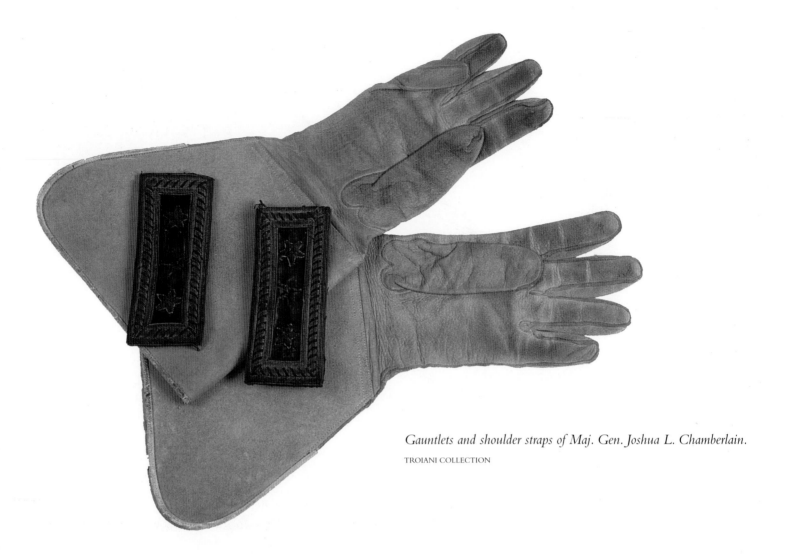

Gauntlets and shoulder straps of Maj. Gen. Joshua L. Chamberlain.
TROIANI COLLECTION

mer enemy, and one Federal soldier recalled, "It was a proud, but sad scene, and our men felt a soldier's sympathy for their brave antagonists."

Once this group had finished its task and marched out of the Union ranks, the Federals cleared the road of equipment and performed the ceremony again with the next group. The ceremony lasted from early in the morning until midafternoon. Close to 24,000 Confederate infantrymen yieldied their trappings that day before beginning the long journey home. Remembering the event, one Southerner recalled: "Someone in the blue line broke the silence and called for three cheers for the last brigade to surrender . . . but for us this soldierly generosity was more than we could bear. Many of the grizzled veterans wept like women, and my own eyes were blind as my voice was dumb." Another wrote: "We suffered no insult in any way from any of our enemies. No other army in the world would have been so considerate of a foe."

In the four years of the war, more than 618,000 Americans gave their lives along the dusty road that led to Appomattox. It all came to an end with the victor and vanquished facing each other one last time.

CHRISTOPHER M. CALKINS

ARTIST COMMENTS

This was one of those situations where there were few angles from which the viewer could see everything important at once. I traveled to Appomattox to survey the site personally.

Original items survive from both generals involved, including Gordon's coat and Chamberlain's hat, sword, ornate yellow leather-trimmed horse equipage, and boots. The shoulder straps that Chamberlain wore that very day are in my collection. All of these items were incorporated into the painting. An original flag of the 32nd Massachusetts from a private collection served as the model for the guide flag.